A President in Our Midst

A President in Our Midst

Franklin Delano Roosevelt in Georgia

KAYE LANNING MINCHEW

Enjoy FDR!

Kaye Lanning Minchew

Published in association with the Georgia Humanities Council

The University of Georgia Press ATHENS

Published in part with generous support from the
Norman and Emmy Lou Illges Foundation

Paperback edition, 2017
© 2016 by the University of Georgia Press
Athens, Georgia 30602
www.ugapress.org

Designed by Erin Kirk New
Set in New Caledonia
Printed and bound by Thomson-Shore, Inc.

The paper in this book meets the guidelines for
permanence and durability of the Committee on
Production Guidelines for Book Longevity of the
Council on Library Resources.

Most University of Georgia Press titles are available from
popular e-book vendors

Printed in the United States of America
21 20 19 18 17 P 5 4 3 2 1

The Library of Congress has cataloged the hardcover edition
of this book as follows:

Minchew, Kaye Lanning, author.
   A president in our midst : Franklin Delano Roosevelt in
Georgia / Kaye Lanning Minchew.
     vii, 270 pages : illustrations ; 22 x 26 cm
   Includes bibliographical references (pages 251–255) and index.
   ISBN 978-0-8203-4918-3 (hardcover : alk. paper)
1. Roosevelt, Franklin D. (Franklin Delano), 1882–1945—
Travel—Georgia. 2. Presidents—United States—Biography.
3. Warm Springs (Ga.)—History—20th century. 4. Warm Springs
(Ga.)—Biography. 5. Presidents—Travel—Georgia. I. Title.
   E807.M55 2016
   973.917092—dc23
                              2015032576
Paperback ISBN 978-0-8203-5299-2

CONTENTS

ACKNOWLEDGMENTS

I had the privilege of serving as the executive director of the Troup County Historical Society and Archives from 1985 to 2015. In those early years, we had a new archive with twenty or more great photographs of Franklin Delano Roosevelt in our collections. Because LaGrange is located less than an hour from Warm Springs, many local residents could share stories about having seen him. I was fortunate to be able to interview some of those people. I also grew up in a North Carolina family that loved FDR. In the 1970s, the only picture I can remember my grandfather having on his walls was one of FDR!

I am indebted to many people for their support. Kevin Shirley of LaGrange College and Jamil Zainaldin of the Georgia Humanities Council were particularly encouraging. John Inscoe, history professor at the University of Georgia; Mike Shaddix, archivist at Roosevelt Warm Springs Institute; Robin Glass of the Little White House; Barbara Schaffer, producer of *A Poor Man's Friend*; and Charlene Baxter at the Lewis Library at LaGrange College have been very helpful. I greatly appreciate the assistance of archivists across Georgia and at the Franklin D. Roosevelt Library in Hyde Park for their tremendous assistance. Special thanks to Harriett Keith and Earl Marsh. James Patrick Allen, Elizabeth Crowley, and John Joerschke at UGA Press have been very helpful, along with copyeditor Barbara Wojhoski. Members of the Lanning and Minchew families and close friends in LaGrange have shared the excitement and stress of the project. The continuing support and encouragement of my husband, Greg Minchew, helps make it all possible. Thank you all!

A President in Our Midst

INTRODUCTION

Franklin Delano Roosevelt "discovered" Warm Springs, Georgia, and its beneficial warm waters in 1924 and quickly grew to love the state and its people. He returned many times in the next twenty-one years. Citizens welcomed him as their adopted son. They saw him at play, at work, and at the steering wheel on drives down local roads. They quickly grew to think of the New Yorker as a friend and hero and one of their own. Georgians embraced Roosevelt as a regular man and enabled him to be elected president of the United States.

The water at Warm Springs bubbles out of nearby Pine Mountain, one of several quartzite ridges running through west central Georgia, maintaining an average temperature of about eighty-eight degrees. According to legend, Native Americans came to recover from sickness and injury in the area's healing waters long before white settlers arrived.

In 1920, Franklin D. Roosevelt seemed to have it all. Despite running for vice president on the losing Democratic ticket with James F. Cox, his political star was rising. His own career already bore a strong resemblance to that of his fifth cousin and his wife, Eleanor's, uncle, Theodore Roosevelt, the twenty-sixth president of the United States. Franklin and Theodore both had served in the New York legislature and as assistant secretary of the U.S. Navy. But in August 1921, Franklin contracted polio, apparently during a summer trip to a Boy Scout camp in New York State (he was president of the Boy Scout Foundation of Greater New York). He fell seriously ill days later during a family vacation at Campobello, Maine. The disease dealt a huge blow to the father of five. Overnight, the tall, aristocratic New Yorker became dependent on others in most aspects of life, and he never again walked or got out of bed without assistance.

For the next few years, Roosevelt poured his energies into recuperating and relearning to walk. At the time, doctors knew relatively little about polio and its treatment. Many victims spent their days in back bedrooms. Indeed, Sara Roosevelt, Franklin's mother, wanted him to go home to Hyde Park, New York, to be a "squire" and preside over the family's country estate of Springwood. Instead, Roosevelt sought treatment in Massachusetts and spent time in the waters of the South Atlantic off the Florida coast. At times, he suffered from such deep depression that he rarely got out of bed before noon.[1]

During his first visit to Warm Springs in the fall of 1924, Roosevelt felt that his legs improved more after spending time in the warm waters than they had the entire time since he had contracted polio. Between then and 1945, Roosevelt visited Georgia and Warm Springs forty-one times. In the early years, his visits focused on exercising at the pool and absorbing the strong rays of the sun. He generally visited every spring in late March and April and again in the fall, arriving in time to spend Thanksgiving with patients at what became the Warm Springs Institute. He quickly grew to love the people and easily made friends with area residents. During those years, he changed from an aristocratic Harvard graduate to a man who struggled to overcome the effects of a ravaging disease and could identify with people in need. He also took on a new role helping others. He became "Doc Roosevelt" at Warm Springs.

At Warm Springs he learned and perfected visual tricks such as leaning against cars or walking with his arm on a son's elbow to appear strong and able in public, though not everyone believed what they saw. Following his nomination and election as Democratic governor of New York in 1928, Roosevelt endured veiled threats from political opponents to reveal his physical disabilities. These verbal jabs added fuel to his desire to appear fit. As the leading contender for the Democratic presidential nomination in 1932, he knew his record as governor, assistant secretary of the navy during World War I, and state representative would indicate his abilities to govern. Now he and his allies launched a concerted effort to show Americans who knew he had suffered from polio that he was physically capable of being the president of the United States.

Roosevelt's second home in Georgia provided the perfect backdrop for this campaign to be seen as an active man. There he sought both improved health and rest from the rigors of everyday life. Like other active, healthy people on vacation, Roosevelt spent days fishing, hunting, horseback riding, and visiting with golfers. He also harbored plans to develop Warm Springs into both a treatment center and a resort for the wealthy. People could come, enjoy the springs, build cottages, and golf or play tennis. He wanted people, especially wealthy northerners, to come to the area. Roosevelt and supporters built a nine-hole golf course, and people came and stayed, but they were generally the families of polio victims. Warm Springs's role in treating both everyday people and wealthy patients continued over the years.

Photographs of a physically active President Roosevelt, whether golfing, fishing, or hunting, are rare. Even photos of him playing with children became scarcer, though he continued to be photographed visiting with young polio victims. Certainly, as president of the United States, he had less free time than ever before. More significantly, the urgency of showing him as an active, healthy man had lessened.

Thanks to national media coverage, public appearances, and radio addresses such as his famous fireside chats, Americans felt they knew their president. Photographs of Roosevelt from 1933 until he died in 1945, as well as oral history interviews and newspaper articles of the day, reveal a public speaker or a person meeting with advisors, family, or friends. Even photographs of him visiting with polio patients in wheelchairs or on crutches present him as a healthy man standing or sitting in a regular chair. He gave opponents few opportunities to depict him as disabled or handicapped. On a larger level, he did not want the United States to appear as failing in health—economically, socially, or as a world power. He wanted to be a symbol of American power.

Roosevelt came to Georgia for twenty-one years, one-third of his life—years when he went from being a former vice-presidential candidate suffering from the effects of a severe case of polio to being president of the United States and one of the world's most powerful leaders. From the first days, his friends and neighbors in Warm Springs and Georgia welcomed him with open arms. They did not always agree with the man or his policies, but they were always happy to see him when he visited his second home.

Though he spent most of his time in Georgia at Warm Springs, Roosevelt played an important role in the state's political affairs. During his initial visit in 1924, he

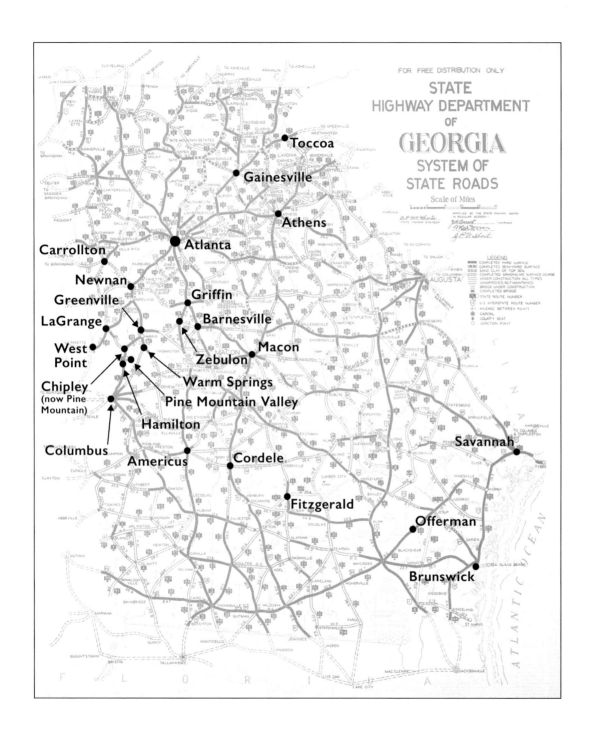

STATE
HIGHWAY DEPARTMENT
OF
GEORGIA
SYSTEM OF
STATE ROADS

Scale of Miles

Toccoa

Gainesville

Athens

Atlanta

Carrollton

Newnan

Greenville

LaGrange

Griffin

Barnesville

West
Point

Macon

Zebulon

Chipley
(now Pine
Mountain)

Warm Springs

Pine Mountain Valley

Hamilton

Columbus

Americus

Cordele

Savannah

Fitzgerald

Offerman

Brunswick

criticized Governor Clifford Walker for speaking at a KKK "Konvention." In the 1930s, Roosevelt served as honorary cochair of the state's bicentennial commission and later battled with Governor Eugene Talmadge and Senator Walter George. Finally, trips during World War II often focused on visits to military bases at Fort Benning and Fort Oglethorpe, where he saw men and women training for armed service. Over the years, he spoke at Sunday schools, addressed civic clubs, made graduation addresses to seventh graders and university seniors, and conferred with the mayors of Georgia cities and the governors of the southern states. As a good politician seeking elective office, he rode in parades, kissed babies, accepted flowers from pretty girls, and greeted people by their first names.

Roosevelt spent much of his time in Georgia writing letters and meeting with advisors. He had many visitors with whom he discussed a wide variety of topics, including affairs in the Middle East and Cuba, rural electrification, and efforts to purge the U.S. Senate of Democrats who often voted against him. He met with campaign advisors and worked on fund-raising for his campaign. He wrote columns for local newspapers and studied the need for new highways and post offices. He drove around the Georgia countryside in open cars, stopped for soft drinks at country stores, spoke to neighbors, and had picnics. He gave some major speeches in Georgia, especially the call for "bold, persistent experimentation" speech of May 1932.

Photographs made of Roosevelt during his visits to Georgia between 1924 and 1945, considered along with interviews of people who remember him, reveal several fairly distinct periods. The first centered on his efforts to recover from polio and to develop Warm Springs as a treatment center. The second consisted of a campaign to show Georgians and the nation that he enjoyed robust health and could handle any job. The third showed him coming to Georgia to rest from the rigors of the presidency as he led the country through the Depression while also dealing with other pressing issues of the day. The Warm Springs Foundation continued to expand as the fight against polio became a national cause. During the fourth period, which started in the late 1930s, the adoration and respect Georgians felt for their adopted son began to wane somewhat when he tried to tell them how to vote and run their businesses. In the fifth era, as commander in chief of a nation at war, Roosevelt had little time to spend in Georgia and, unfortunately, little time to enjoy the beneficial, healing effects of Warm Springs.

Roosevelt benefited immeasurably from his time in Georgia. The waters at Warm Springs greatly helped his recovery from polio and gave him reason to believe he could overcome its physical damage. In 1932, his successful fight with polio helped make him an electable presidential candidate during the worst depression the nation had ever suffered. He had spent years in Georgia meeting regular people who had been suffering from a hurting economy. Had he not contracted polio and dealt with the consequences of the disease, Roosevelt would have been a much less attractive candidate to many voters, especially during the hard economic times of 1932. With polio and with the friendship of Georgians, Roosevelt connected with the common man during the nation's worst economic crisis. His time in Georgia enabled him to become the thirty-second president of the United States.

Roosevelt died at his Georgia home in April 1945. He had just entered his fourth term as the highest elected official in the land a few months earlier. The United States and its allies were still fighting World War II. With him in Warm Springs were two cousins, a portrait painter, and Lucy Rutherford, the woman who had almost broken up his marriage almost three decades earlier. Throughout the years and various, difficult challenges, Roosevelt remained a neighbor, a friend, and a president in our midst.

CHAPTER 1

Discovering Warm Springs and Georgia

FRANKLIN ROOSEVELT first visited Georgia on November 18, 1913, touring Brunswick as an assistant secretary of the navy in President Woodrow Wilson's administration. Twelve years later, he described that trip to Brunswick and Biloxi, Mississippi. The navy needed a port to house small vessels and equipment on the Atlantic Seaboard somewhere between Norfolk and New Orleans. "Speaking of the Navy, I am reminded of a trip . . . I made . . . soon after I went to the Navy Department in 1913. The good people of Brunswick, Ga. and of Biloxie [*sic*], Miss. were anxious to have the Federal Government establish naval stations in their harbors. . . . Brunswick, I remember chiefly, for the possum banquet they gave me—every known variety of possum—cooked in every known variety of style. I had them all."[1]

The dinner took place at the Oglethorpe Hotel. It was the second annual "dollar dinner" sponsored by the Brunswick Board of Trade. In addition to possum, the menu featured oysters on the half shell, turkey and dressing, and other items celebrating Georgia Products Day. Over 225 guests attended. Newspaper and civic leaders viewed the dinner as important for the "future growth and prosperity of the city." The *Brunswick News* considered the evening part of the "up-to-date movement for a bigger and better Brunswick."[2]

Roosevelt arrived in Brunswick about noon and left the next day. His wife, Eleanor, and cousin Laura Delano accompanied him. His reservations included one double and one single room. In the afternoon, the Roosevelt party and a group from the Board of Trade rode the steamer *Atlantic* through the harbor area and stopped at Jekyll Island. This was Roosevelt's only known visit to the island, which hosted many Republican leaders through the years. The next day, the group motored around Brunswick and its industrial area, which included naval products companies. In summing up the trip on November 20, 1913, the *Brunswick News* thought Roosevelt had all but promised more naval activity there. "There is no doubt that the secretary was surprised at the matchless harbor which he found here in Brunswick." Roosevelt had given Georgians their first glimpse of his charm and his political style. By chance, Laura Delano would also be a guest during Roosevelt's last visit in April 1945.

A few decades later, the U.S. Army built a base near Brunswick at St. Mary's. King's Bay Ocean Terminal opened in 1958. Then in 1975, the U.S. Navy took over operations and opened the Kings Bay submarine base.

This photograph shows William Jennings Bryan (light suit), President Woodrow Wilson (dark jacket, light slacks), Josephus Daniels (just visible between Bryan and Wilson), Roosevelt (far right on platform), and others gathered for a Flag Day ceremony at the State, War, and Navy Building in Washington, D.C., on June 14, 1913.

DURING A FAMILY VACATION at Campobello Island, off the coast of Maine, in the summer of 1921, Roosevelt fell victim to infantile paralysis—the dreaded polio disease, which had killed, paralyzed, and maimed victims for centuries. He was physically exhausted when he contracted the disease, which quickly became more severe. Making matters worse, doctors initially misdiagnosed the symptoms.

By the 1920s polio had been known for several centuries, but treatment remained disorganized. Although medical care as a whole was becoming more professional during this period, and more doctors were now graduates of rigorous medical schools, they had few guidelines for advising polio patients. Also the disease affected each patient differently. Experts in the care of polio were usually doctors and nurses who had worked with victims of earlier epidemics.

Roosevelt spent several years seeking treatment and exercising in hopes of walking without braces or crutches. When a doctor recommended that the former Democratic vice presidential nominee seek warm water to strengthen his wasted leg muscles, a friend of Roosevelt, native Georgian George Foster Peabody, suggested that he visit Warm Springs. The waters there flow at a rate of eight hundred gallons per minute with the temperature remaining constant at about eighty-eight degrees. The minerals provide buoyancy, and the stable warm temperature does not tire swimmers as much as colder or hotter water. Peabody owned part interest in the resort and knew that one young man, Louis Joseph, had arrived at Warm Springs lame in the early 1920s and left walking after spending days in the warm, healing waters of the springs.

The healing powers of Warm Springs had been recognized for centuries. Reportedly, Native Americans wounded in tribal wars had visited there in the days before European explorers and settlers arrived. A resort had been located in the area since the late 1820s, and nineteenth-century visitors included nationally known figures such as Henry Clay and John C. Calhoun. However, the 120-room Victorian-style Meriwether Inn (shown in the photograph), which was built in 1889, and the nearby cabins that greeted Roosevelt upon his arrival had fallen into disrepair. Roosevelt later described the pools and the inn: "I wish you had seen this building ten years ago. It was a perfectly good down-at-the-heel summer resort and nothing else. . . . It was in awful condition."[3]

The William Hart family of Columbus, Georgia, shared their cottage with Roosevelt during his first few visits. Roosevelt never stayed at the inn, considering it a firetrap that would be difficult to exit in an emergency. The inn later housed patients and guests of the Warm Springs Foundation and served as an administrative building before it was demolished in 1934. Roosevelt declared, "Those of us who have memories of the old Inn and of the old Georgia Warm Springs, we can still cherish those old memories and still be devoutly thankful that the old Inn is gone."[4]

LOCATED SIXTY MILES southwest of Atlanta—and a similar distance from Columbus and Macon—Warm Springs stood ten miles from the nearest paved road in 1924. Roosevelt found the countryside interesting and had great hope for the healing powers of the springs. He wrote his mother in October 1924: "We are here safely. . . . I spent over an hour in the pool this a.m. and it is really wonderful . . . you can be sure I am really taking all the precautions of a cure and getting every minute's worth out of it."[5] During this first visit, he went riding in an open car through the rural countryside with Tom Loyless, the operator of the Meriwether Inn. He noted how many peach orchards grew in the area and how neglect and poverty affected many people in the region. (Nine decades later, the area still boasts several fine peach orchards.)

He wrote Eleanor after she returned to New York: "Dearest E, It is just a week since you left. . . . The legs are really improving a great deal. . . . This is really a discovery of a place and there is no doubt that I've got to do it some more."[6]

Henry H. Revill, editor of the *Meriwether Vindicator*, described "A Distinguished Guest within Our Gates" on October 24, 1924. "Hon. Franklin D. Roosevelt, of New York, is a guest within our gates. Broken in health, he has come to our own Warm Springs, to bathe in its health giving fount, to enjoy our blue skies and bright sunshine; to listen to the soughing of our pines. . . . He is a great statesman whose superb talents have won for him a place in the sun. Ere he leaves old Meriwether for his far away home . . . may his body become as stalwart as his great mind."

AS MANAGER of Al Smith's campaign for president of the United States in 1924, Roosevelt appeared at the Democratic National Convention, nominated Smith to be the Democratic candidate for president, and made his first speech on the new medium of radio. As he continued to seek relief from the damage polio had caused his body, he traveled first to Florida and then to Georgia. Just before he left New York for Florida, he resigned from the law firm of Langdon P. Marvin and Erenville T. Emmett.[7]

When Roosevelt first traveled to Warm Springs, many people in the United States enjoyed the prosperous times of the Roaring Twenties. Many Georgians, however, suffered from an economic depression caused by the boll weevil and a decline in farm prices. Despite the hardships, people made time for recreation. Trains filled with people arrived in Warm Springs and pulled up in front of the warm-water pools. The trains would then wait to take these visitors home later in the day.

The Warm Springs area suffered another blow in 1924 when a storm hit the area, destroying homes and injuring several people. On May 9, H. Inman Talbot, secretary of the Warm Springs Relief Society, which organized after the storm, stated in the *Meriwether Vindicator*, "I can truthfully state that the distress is far greater than estimated at first. Most of the victims are people who were in rather destitute circumstances before their misfortune . . . in several instances, entire families, both white and colored are without food, shelter, or clothing." By October, the immediate needs of these people had been met, but the effects of the storm, including damaged trees and homes, would have been visible to visitors.

THOUGH ROOSEVELT liked to think of himself as just one of the people, his dress reflected his upper-class upbringing in Hyde Park, New York. He had attended Groton Prep School, Harvard University, and Columbia Law School. He usually wore a suit and tie with pince-nez glasses perched on his nose—a trademark he shared with his fifth cousin, Theodore Roosevelt—and used a long cigarette holder.

Roosevelt's presence in Warm Springs drew immediate attention from the press, thanks to the efforts of former newspaperman Tom Loyless, who had published papers in Augusta and Columbus, and George Foster Peabody. Both men were determined to breathe new life into the resort. On October 3, 1924, the *LaGrange Graphic* carried a story announcing that Roosevelt and his wife would be arriving that day. He was expected to return to New York in early November for the presidential election and would then come back to the South for an extended stay. The article noted, "A great deal of interest is attached to Mr. Roosevelt's proposed visit to Warm Springs due to his prominence. He is one of the leaders in the democratic party."

Three months later, Loyless wrote an article in the *Macon Daily Telegraph* mentioning Roosevelt as the next presidential nominee. In his As Loyless Sees It column on January 14, 1925, he reported that he had visited with Roosevelt in New York.

> He is as fine and cheerful and energetic as ever, with all of his unfortunate affliction. . . . No man could make the fight he is making and not win. . . . He told me, by the way that he doesn't want me, or anyone else, to be talking about him in connection with the next Democratic Presidential nomination. Says, in the first place, he is not a candidate and doesn't expect to be; and, moreover, such talk may tend to discredit and discount all that he is, sincerely, and unselfishly, trying to do to harmonize and reorganize the Democratic party.[8]

WHEN ROOSEVELT started going to Warm Springs, the South had already entered into a serious economic depression. Southern farmers depended on cotton as their major source of cash even though the boll weevil increasingly destroyed crops and low prices limited profits. Some farmers gave up on the land and moved into towns to work in the textile mills. In the mostly segregated South, blacks found few employment opportunities, and many opted for the promise of a better life in northern cities like Chicago, Detroit, and Cleveland. Farm housing often consisted of tenant shacks that lacked indoor plumbing, electricity, and modern conveniences of the day.

In a press conference held at the Little White House in 1934, Roosevelt addressed the issue when he quoted a friend and cotton manufacturer: "Cason Callaway takes pride in saying that he has thoroughly investigated agriculture in Georgia. You could grow anything in Georgia except corn and cotton, and yet those are the two things that the state grows." He went on to say: "Any of you who live in, let us say, a prosperous rural section of the State of New York, if you come down here into the average rural section of any of the Southern states, you are immediately struck by what looks like poverty, real poverty. . . . In the first place, you have the Negro problem. In the second place, you have what they used to call the 'poor white' problem. The standard of living is absolutely and totally different from what it is in the prosperous areas of the West or of the North."[9]

Henry Wallace, the midwesterner who served as Roosevelt's secretary of agriculture from 1933 to 1940 and as vice president from 1941 to 1945, first visited Georgia after the 1932 election. "On my way to Warm Springs, I was utterly amazed and appalled at the red gashed hillsides, at the unkempt cabins, some of them without windows or doors. It was a situation, it seemed to me with an Iowa farm background that was almost unbelievable."[10]

WHEN ROOSEVELT arrived in Georgia in 1924, the state had begun to modernize, but slowly. School systems often held classes for just a few months, and many people could not read or write. More and more individuals owned cars and trucks, yet the majority of roads remained unpaved and travel with automobiles remained difficult. As efforts increased to improve roadways, John Whitley and his Whitley Construction Company in LaGrange started winning major paving contracts in West Georgia and throughout the state. Whitley also developed close friendships with Roosevelt and Georgia political leader Eugene Talmadge. Whitley and Roosevelt may have been friends in Florida in the early 1920s, and Roosevelt is thought to have stayed at his fishing camp in northern Troup County.[11]

CHAPTER 2

Fighting Polio

ROOSEVELT had long been physically active, though he had never been a great athlete in his youth, partly due to his small size. He played football and managed the baseball team at Groton. As an adult, he grew to six feet, one and a half inches, and his ideal weight hovered around 175 pounds. Even while recovering from the debilitating effects of polio, he went sailing off the coast of Florida for two consecutive winters. Roosevelt believed that the warm sun boosted his health. On his first visit to Warm Springs, he thought that his legs improved for the first time since he had contracted polio. He also developed significant upper-body strength, which contrasted with his thin, useless legs. During this visit in the mid-1920s and later ones, Roosevelt spent mornings in warm pool waters fed by the natural springs. At Warm Springs, he could do two things he greatly enjoyed doing: swimming and driving a car. The swimming pool with its warm waters helped win Roosevelt over.[1]

T. J. "Jess" Long later remembered Roosevelt's first visit to Warm Springs. He and other local residents greeted the former vice presidential candidate at the railroad depot. No ramp existed to help Roosevelt get off the train, so locals assisted. "George Blount and I formed a saddle seat with our crossed hands and carried him to a car. He called me Jess from that day until he died. He was a wonderful man, a friend to everyone."[2]

ROOSEVELT AND FELLOW VISITORS gathered in full business dress at the pool at Warm Springs, probably in the spring of 1925. Dr. Leroy Hubbard sits on the floor and Missy LeHand, Roosevelt's longtime secretary, sits second to the left of Roosevelt. The previous fall, on October 17, he told *Columbus Ledger* reporters that he was improving and was "confident of complete recovery eventually." Nine days later, Cleburne Gregory wrote in the *Atlanta Journal* that Roosevelt "swims, dives, uses swimming rings and horizontal bars and then bathes in the sun." FDR declared that he had gained great physical benefits by being there, "literally swimming himself back to health and strength at Warm Springs, Georgia." The article went on to state that Roosevelt did not pity himself. He knew that he had been hit hard by the disease and recognized that the warm waters allowed him to exercise and stay in the water for two or more hours at a time. Beyond that, he gave the Georgia sunshine credit for the improvement in his health.

In concluding his article, Gregory mentioned Roosevelt's unflagging optimism. Gregory felt certain that this positive attitude would help restore Roosevelt's health and bring him success for years in the future.

When Roosevelt returned to New York in the fall of 1924, he formed a law partnership with Basil O'Connor, but he continued to think about Warm Springs. In his first "Roosevelt Says" editorial in the *Macon Telegraph* on April 16, 1925, Roosevelt gave a chatty description about how Gregory's article generated interest in Warm Springs. During the 1924 visit, Tom Loyless had introduced him to Gregory. Roosevelt recalled, "We talked about health and crops and politics. . . . Then came the newspaper clippings—whole sheets of them—Sunday supplements, illustrations—from every paper between here and Seattle, Wash. There I was, large as life, living proof that Warm Springs, Georgia had cured me of 57 different varieties of ailments . . . it started a flood of correspondence, which hasn't reached its crest yet."

When the resort reopened in the spring of 1925, after being closed for the winter, polio victims arrived by train seeking to improve their health. With no doctors at the complex, Roosevelt stepped in to help patients with walking and underwater exercises. The treatment was not necessarily new or different, but he and a local doctor began to develop muscle charts and became more systematic in the treatment of polio. Roosevelt and eighteen or so other polio victims soon began commenting on "the Warm Springs Spirit." Gaiety and laughter made their struggles a little easier. In the mid-1920s, Warm Springs lacked luxuries. The roads were unpaved, the Meriwether Inn was showing its age, and funds for continuing therapy at Warm Springs were uncertain. Patients and guests nonetheless had fun, and everyone contributed as much as possible to the day-to-day operations.[3]

ROOSEVELT FIRST BUILT a cottage for himself at Warm Springs in 1926–27. Upon completion of the project, he wrote his mother: "The new cottage is too sweet, really very good in every way, the woodwork covering all walls and ceilings a great success." This cottage, which later came to be known as McCarthy Cottage, had wide horizontal pine boards in the living room that were oiled, not stained or painted. Roosevelt stayed there until 1932, when he built the Little White House, designed by Henry J. Toombs. Leighton McCarthy, a close friend of Roosevelt's who served as Canadian ambassador to the United States from 1941 to 1944, purchased the 1926 cottage after Roosevelt moved into his new home. McCarthy's son John was also a victim of infantile paralysis. In the Little White House, Roosevelt reversed two major exterior features of the first home by enabling wheelchair access through the front door and placing the deck in the rear.

According to Toombs, Roosevelt built the cottage in 1926 "partially to induce other patients and friends to move there." Toombs designed the home and many other buildings at the Warm Springs Foundation, in keeping with Roosevelt's goal of creating a place of "informality and truly languid southern atmosphere." In 1937, Roosevelt declared that despite all the changes and new buildings that had been constructed, "I don't want anybody to think that this is a completed Warm Springs. We have only just started. . . . Every year that I come down here I go over blueprints. . . . Well, those blueprints show us the Warm Springs of the future only so far as we today can analyze."[4]

After Roosevelt's death, Toombs recalled that he had "a strong, if untutored, architectural sense. He was quick to grasp, to see relationship in plans, and fertile in suggestions and ideas. He loved to build. Any project, new or in progress, excited his interests."[5] Roosevelt worked closely with the Cuthbert, Georgia, native on these projects. Indeed, he once told the American Institute of Architects that if he were a young man, he would consider becoming an architect.

James Roosevelt later reflected on the development of Warm Springs with Rexford Tugwell: "I think the thing that finally got Father interested was that . . . he loved to plan and to dream of making things that he planned to grow and here was a wonderful opportunity to build those very things he loved."[6] The photo shows the cottage in the summer of 2000 with front porch screening. The house burned to the ground on August 9, 2011, apparently due to a lightning strike.

ROOSEVELT AND AN UNIDENTIFIED MAN, probably Dr. Leroy Hubbard, swim in front of the old dressing rooms at Warm Springs in 1926 or 1927. Dr. Hubbard came to Warm Springs from the New York Board of Health to oversee the treatment of patients. Except when speaking to his doctors and therapists, Roosevelt did not discuss hardships caused by his polio and never wrote about his problems until 1945. He surrounded himself with positive people and liked to have friends with him when eating, swimming, and driving.

After reading Cleburne Gregory's article, polio patient Fred Botts came to Warm Springs in 1925 and started walking with crutches after a few weeks. He described his first mornings at the pools: "Soon Mr. Roosevelt's cheery 'Good Morning!' sounded on the air and in a few minutes he had joined us in the pool. At once we were told and shown a series of exercises he had worked out. It was 'Catch hold of the bar this way——now——swing——in and out——Hard! Harder! that's it——that's fine! Now——again, this way!' . . . It was all along the line of lending to the affected limbs and muscles the normal activities as near as possible. We were told to concentrate hard on every action and movement."[7]

Roosevelt quickly "sold" his early visitors on his vision of what Warm Springs could become. Botts reported that "a few mornings later Mr. Roosevelt, having gathered us around him in the general round-table discussion, deftly made inference as to what the future might hold for us. . . . We needed a private patients pool and we needed equipment . . . and we needed doctors and nurses! What glorious news."[8] Botts went on to work as registrar at the foundation for many years.

ON APRIL 29, 1926, Roosevelt purchased 1,200 acres of land in Warm Springs. He paid George Foster Peabody $195,000 for the land, monies that represented two-thirds of Roosevelt's net worth. In 1939, at the dedication of Peabody's portrait at Georgia Hall, Dr. James J. Johnson stated that Peabody had purchased the property "with the idea in mind of turning it into a Recreational Park and presenting it to his native State—Georgia." Regardless of his intentions, Peabody made a nice profit on the sale, having paid about half that amount a few years earlier. Roosevelt later bought additional land bringing the total to 2,500 acres. His purchase included the resort, springs, pools, hotel, and cottages.[9]

Roosevelt made the purchase with the mixed blessing of his wife, Eleanor. She wrote him on May 4, 1926: "I know you love creative work, my only feeling is that Georgia is somewhat distant for you to keep in touch with what is really a big undertaking. . . . Don't be discouraged by me; I have great confidence in your extraordinary interest and enthusiasm."[10] Eleanor wrote as a practical wife. She knew Warm Springs would require much attention and money, plus she never really felt comfortable there. Race relations and the fact that blacks worked mostly in subservient positions as cooks or aides also made her uncomfortable.

He wrote Eleanor on October 13, after she had visited Warm Springs: "I miss you a lot. . . . I know you were really interested in seeing what I think is a very practical good to which this place can be put

and you needn't worry about my losing a fortune in it, for every step is being planned either to pay for itself or to make a profit on."[11]

The people of Georgia reacted to the purchase with enthusiasm. Editors of the *Meriwether Vindicator* wrote: "It is worthwhile to have Franklin D. Roosevelt as a part of our good old county. He is a great big, clean-cut, outstanding boy, with the brain of a giant. He radiates sunshine. . . . We are glad he has bought some dirt here and we are deeply obsessed with the conviction that he is to be a potent factor in Meriwether's growth. . . . He is just as much at ease with boys in overalls as with those in tuxedoes."[12]

Between 1926 and 1939, Roosevelt averaged two visits a year. Here in the spring of 1928, he was photographed in the midst of his afternoon routine: checking business files, answering correspondence, and reading newspapers to stay current on world affairs.

IN APRIL 1927, young Paul Hasbrouck came to Warm Springs for six weeks of treatment. In letters to his parents, he commented on his days. "Here the weather has been perfect *July*. Not excessively hot, but pretty warm for any coat in the afternoon." He reported that meals were "done southern style, no meal call, but we appear about 8, 1, and 6:15 and are served as we come." Meals featured lamb, roast beef, chicken, or other meats. The amount of construction and work being done in preparation for summer amazed him; workers were remodeling cottages and the inn, building a new pool, and laying out the golf course. Every morning, except Sundays, patients went to the pool. They usually drove their own cars or rode with staff. He remarked, "The pools are not so far from the cottages, but there is a steep, rough hill down which a person must be pretty mobile to walk." He liked the pools' warmth and noted, "All about the place, there is a perceptible soft sulphurous (I suppose) odor. . . . It tastes, in the main, just 'soft.' Its temperature is mildly warm to the touch, and the whole pool stays so mild that today I stayed in for what seemed like a very long time without having any desire to get out."[13]

His first week that April included a swimming party at 8:30 p.m. on Friday. Hasbrouck reported that the guests stayed in the warm waters for forty-five minutes that night despite the chilly temperature. Other evenings, they played bridge or chess with fires to warm them. Following a drive to nearby Greenville and Durand, he stated: "There are no paved roads at all. The width is fairly good, however, the roads are just sandy dust, even after a good rain. . . . The country is much the same here, whatever way you go. Hilly, with small fields of the red soil, a varied sprinkling of woods with beautiful pine clumps predominant, and with typical southern shanty

everywhere. The fields are small. We passed some oats, more cotton fields with sprouts just visible, one field of peas, and frequent fine peach orchards."[14] Hasbrouck noted that Warm Springs seemed isolated from the rest of the world, and he appreciated letters and clippings from home. Dr. Hubbard often shared his copy of Atlanta newspapers or the *New York Times*.

On May 1, he visited one of Roosevelt's favorite places. "This afternoon we took a truly beautiful drive, to the Knob, about ten miles to the south. The road led up along the ridges of pine mountains . . . through some of the largest peach orchards in the country, which seemed to be located on the top of the world. The Knob is the abrupt end and highest point of the ridge. . . . The views were wide and beautiful all along the route, and there were many wild flowers in the woods. . . . While I wouldn't want to take this trip in the old Ford again, I am glad to have been there once, and to have had a wide look around."[15]

DURING THE 1920S AND 1930S, Roosevelt played a central role in the development of Warm Springs Institute and the care of its patients. As early as spring of 1925, before he purchased the land, Roosevelt assumed responsibility for many of the resort's operations as the health of manager Tom Loyless failed. He became "Dr. Roosevelt" as he sought to improve the health of all polio patients at Warm Springs and wrote columns for the *Macon Daily Telegraph* as he took over yet another job from the manager. He contributed nine "Roosevelt Says" articles to the paper during his spring 1925 visit to Georgia. Though never syndicated, the columns appeared in other newspapers across the state. He and Dr. James Johnson, of nearby Manchester, developed a muscle group chart that aided in developing water exercises to strengthen specific areas of the body. Roosevelt also developed a water table that sat twelve inches below the surface of the water for polio patients to use when exercising. Remarkably, the table continued to be used in water therapy for many years. Just as he did in politics, Roosevelt relied on his instincts in the treatment of polio. Under his guidance, the Warm Springs Foundation claimed no miracles or cures but promised better treatment for patients.[16]

When the American Orthopaedic Association held its annual meeting in Atlanta in January 1926, Roosevelt attended the meeting and cornered doctors in hallways to tell them about work being done at Warm Springs. The association formed an advisory committee that worked with Roosevelt. The committee soon recommended establishing a hydrotherapeutic center at Warm Springs. In 1928, the Georgia Warm Springs Foundation became a reality.

The foundation incorporated under Delaware law with Roosevelt as president, his former law partner Basil O'Connor as secretary-treasurer, and Roosevelt's advisor Louis Howe as one of the directors. The foundation emphasized patient care and, secondarily, experimental therapy and treatment. Roosevelt declared the goal of Warm Springs to be "bringing cripples back to some kind of useful activity . . . useful citizenship." Work at Warm Springs concentrated on the "building up of muscles over a period of two years or three or four, or even ten years, so that the individual may become functionally able to get about."[17]

Roosevelt often joined other patients and staff in water games. In the early 1930s, Walter Doyle served as a push boy who worked mostly at the pool. "When we finished with the work at hand, we'd have what we called water polo. It really wasn't water polo; it was 'try to get the ball away from Mr. Roosevelt.' He would sit in the middle of the pool. . . . From the waist down, he was skin and bones, but from the waist up, he was a powerful man. He'd hold that rubber ball high above his head in the air and just dare you to come and get it. Every time I'd get close, he'd take his powerful hands and push me down. When he pushed, you went straight to the bottom of the pool."[18]

In addition to throwing the ball, Roosevelt often made up pool games. Bill Trotter, who grew up in nearby Manchester and swam in the patients' pool because his father and Roosevelt were friends, remembered such games: "What amazed us able-bodied people so much was that you would get into a pool tag game with those folks and they would out swim you, they would really fly, amazing."[19]

THOUGH CALLED INFANTILE PARALYSIS and striking young victims especially hard, polio afflicted people of all ages. Roosevelt himself had been a relatively healthy though exhausted thirty-nine-year-old in 1921 when he visited a Boy Scout camp in New York and then, a couple of days later, went for a swim in the Bay of Fundy off the coast of Maine. Soon he lay paralyzed. For centuries, handicapped patients stayed isolated in hospital wards and back bedrooms, removed from the mainstream of the public. By the 1920s, this attitude, along with medical practices, began to change. In addition to specially developed exercises and trained polio doctors and physiotherapists, patients at Warm Springs enjoyed parties, talent shows, and dinners. Fine china and tablecloths were routinely used in the dining room.

Roosevelt dined at Georgia Hall with some of the younger patients, dressed in their finest clothes for dinner with the president. Frank Cheatham remembered a day in the 1930s: "On the occasion of one of the President's visits to Warm Springs, I was at Warm Springs recovering from surgery in the hospital on campus as were other patients in the hospital. We were not going to be able to attend the luncheon. We were deeply disappointed. We couldn't see our hero, the President of the United States . . . but who should roll into my room one day but the President. He didn't stay long, just made a cheerful greeting and was off to another room . . . visiting every patient in the hospital."[20]

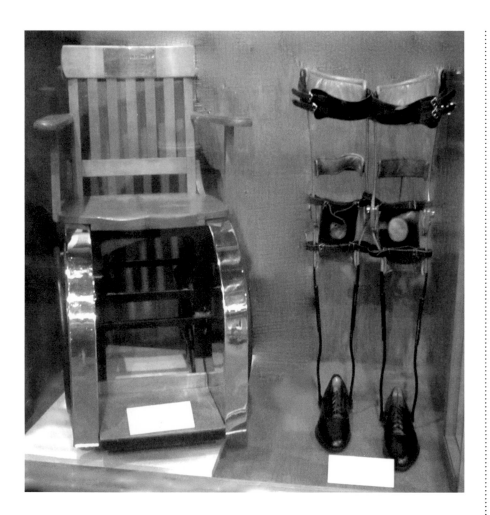

PHOTOGRAPHS OF ROOSEVELT in his wheelchair or wearing his leg braces are extremely rare. More often, he sat or walked with the assistance of an aide or one of his sons. In the fall of 1928, he was elected governor of New York, and many viewed him as the leading Democratic contender for president in four years. From this point on, he tried to minimize his handicap when appearing before the public. In the mid-1920s, he occasionally joked about his lame legs during speeches before quickly changing subjects. Soon his staff had instructions not to mention his condition in correspondence or press releases. On display at the Little White House, a wheelchair that he used and helped design and leg braces offer clues about how Roosevelt moved around each day. He used this wheelchair solely for transportation; he would scoot from the wheelchair to a desk chair, couch, or car seat, but spent little time actually sitting in the wheelchair.[21]

Mary Hudson Veeder once described the disease to fellow physiotherapist Audrey Trowbridge: "Polio is like the aftermath of a tornado. It is the wreckage that is left."[22] Polio affected patients differently and with varying degrees of severity. Some spent a week or more confined to an iron lung for assistance with breathing, while others, like Roosevelt, were fortunate to be able to walk using braces and crutches. Many later suffered from post-polio syndrome, which affects survivors years after the onset of the disease. Much like polio itself, post-polio creates great pain for some victims while barely affecting others.

ENJOYING THE SUN and fresh air are Roosevelt and Dr. C. E. Irwin, a physician at Warm Springs. A native of Georgia, Irwin first worked at Warm Springs under chief surgeon Dr. Michael Hoke and in 1935 became chief surgeon and medical director, positions he held for twenty years. He wrote extensively about the treatment of polio and developed several techniques in orthopedic surgery. Many surgeons trained and interned at Warm Springs, thus spreading the accomplishments of the foundation.

Roosevelt started going to Dowdell's Knob for picnics in the 1920s, and this remained one of his favorite outings for the rest of his life. On an early trip, he broke one of his leg braces as he moved about near the barbecue pit, causing him to fall to the ground. John Riehle, an electrician at the foundation, helped him to a car cushion. Within days, Riehle determined that he could not only repair the brace but also make a much lighter one. Making braces locally saved patients weeks of waiting for braces ordered from distant locations. Riehle went to Children's Hospital in Boston for training and started using aluminum and other metals, which resulted in much lighter braces than had previously been available. The brace shop at Warm Springs Foundation continues to operate and supply patients' needs.

FRANKLIN ROOSEVELT and patients, friends, and staff of the Warm Springs Foundation gathered to watch *Palala Pollo*, a play staged by patients in the early 1930s. Eagerly anticipated by both participants and observers, plays typically followed dinner. Having Roosevelt in the audience added even more excitement to an evening. Such activities helped create the "spirit of Warm Springs." Special activities also occurred throughout the year. For instance, the Fourth of July included fireworks, water carnivals, and pool contests.

In his book *Franklin D. Roosevelt: A Career in Progressive Democracy*—the first biography of Roosevelt—newspaper journalist Ernest Lindley observes: "Warm Springs is a gay place; there are few places gayer. The patients, from two-year olds with their parents to men and women of sixty, eat together. . . . Immediately after breakfast they go to the pools, where the physiotherapists—very attractive young women—massage them and give them exercises underwater. . . . In the evening there are moving pictures and bridge and various other games. . . . The atmosphere of the place is that of a resort rather than of a sanitarium."[23]

Staff and patients at Warm Springs closely followed Roosevelt's political career and were always thrilled to see him. Election nights sometimes featured bonfires plus radio hookups throughout the facilities so that patients and staff could follow vote counts.

ROOSEVELT WORKS WITH Basil "Doc"
O'Connor at McCarthy Cottage in November 1928,
following his election as governor of New York.
Though born into a wealthy family, Roosevelt did
not have unlimited funds. He financed operations at
Warm Springs by developing the property as a treatment center for polio victims. The foundation grew
thanks in part to donations for major expenditures,
such as new buildings. Warm Springs received several high-profile donations after Roosevelt reentered
politics in 1928.

In December 1930, Roosevelt announced, "The
Warm Springs Foundation proposes to raise an
endowment fund which will provide treatment for
patients who are unable to pay for it. . . . It will
make Warm Springs an institution of nationwide
helpfulness."[24] Roosevelt always made certain that
rich and poor and young and old had access to treatment at Warm Springs, though only whites were
treated there until the 1950s.

Roosevelt also used this table and his desk to
work on his stamp collection, a favorite hobby.
On December 11, 1930, he wrote Warren Delano
Robbins, a cousin who served as minister to San
Salvador and later Canada: "It was certainly fine of
you to send me those grand Salvador stamps. As you
know I get real relaxation at Warm Springs from
my stamps and it is splendid help in removing all
thoughts of politics from my musty brain."[25]

ROOSEVELT SPENT many enjoyable hours in the pools at Warm Springs. When swimming, he actively fought his polio. He stood six feet two inches and weighed about 187 pounds. He built great upper-body strength, yet his legs remained thin and totally lacking in muscles.

Louis Howe, Roosevelt's closest political advisor, helped Roosevelt attract financial support for Warm Springs from the business community. Howe recommended development of a chain of resorts from Lake Placid, New York, to Warm Springs with the therapeutic project in Georgia being used to generate interest. They planned to have both a health and rehabilitation center and a resort that would attract visitors from around the country. An article in the *Atlanta Georgian* about the new "Meriwether Reserve" described a year-round resort that would rival Pinehurst and the Carolina mountains by drawing southerners in the summer and eastern visitors during the winter. The plans included a new hotel atop Pine Mountain, two eighteen-hole golf courses, stables, a twenty-five-acre lake for fishing, a quail and game preserve, a dance pavilion, and eating facilities. Financial support for the resort concept might have been lacking or a pragmatic Roosevelt may have decided instead to focus on medical issues after realizing that healthy vacationers in the 1920s resisted sharing facilities with polio victims.[26]

FROM HIS EARLIEST TIME at Warm Springs, Roosevelt divided his days between swimming, sunbathing, and working. In the pregubernatorial days, work consisted of corresponding about political matters, taking care of his law practice, reading, and developing plans for Warm Springs. Though he stayed busy, he had time to explore new ideas, visit with local residents, and catch up on his reading. Rev. W. G. Harry, who later served as a mayor of Warm Springs, recalled being a curious visitor when he first met Roosevelt in 1926. The then North Carolina resident "called on the Foundation one afternoon and was just looking over the new situation that he had developed there." He recalled, "I was in front of the little cottage . . . that was Roosevelt's first cottage. . . . I just walked up and went to the door and he was sitting at his typewriter facing the door—he said come right in. I went in and introduced myself. . . . He insisted that I sit right down and he started from that and he talked to me for one solid hour most enthusiastically about all this country side and what he planned to do and what he expected to do about it."[27]

Roosevelt made every effort to appear physically fit before the public, though not everyone believed what they saw. Following his nomination as the Democratic candidate for governor of New York in 1928, Republicans saluted Roosevelt's leadership while questioning his ability. "He is lauded for his public spirit in accepting the nomination against his personal inclination and the advice of his physician . . . general health excellent, mental capacity and vigor are great. If he cannot walk with entire freedom, the people of this state can make sympathetic allowances for him."[28] Such comments added fuel to Roosevelt's determination to appear fit. Between 1924 and 1928, Roosevelt focused primarily on improving his health but occasionally got involved in local politics. In February 1927, he was guest of honor at a dinner of Georgia officials and Democratic leaders at the Biltmore Hotel in Atlanta. Hollins S. Randolph, head of the 1924 Georgia delegation to the Democratic National Convention, which voted solidly for William G. McAdoo (rather than Al Smith, whom Roosevelt supported), hosted the dinner. The Ku Klux Klan also supported McAdoo in 1924. Randolph reported that Roosevelt was "much improved in health and attribute[d] his improvements to the beneficial effect of the Springs."[29]

IN A RARE PHOTOGRAPH, Roosevelt used crutches as he walked with three other polio patients at Warm Springs. The group worked on the grounds near the Meriwether Inn at Warm Springs. Paul Rogers, a patient who visited in the mid-1920s, recalled treatment in those early days. "We would get out in the yard, and three or four of us would walk and the President would walk—he wasn't President then of course, he wasn't even governor . . . conversations were very general conversations . . . and there were cocktail parties . . . and FDR appeared at a great many of them. . . . It was a joy to have him around at parties . . . everything livened up and everything was swell."[30]

Roosevelt and fellow patients used handrails that were located near one of the cottages to practice walking. Paul Hasbrouck, a fellow Dutchess County resident who sought treatment at Warm Springs in the spring of 1927, wrote to his mother: "Part of the daily program is walking which takes place from 3:00 to 4:00 in the afternoon under the supervision of Miss Mahoney and Dr. Hubbard. The walking is for quality, more than quantity—that is, patients are corrected in the way they walk. The rails are for those, like Mr. Roosevelt, who need something to take hold of on both sides, but the aim is to become independent of the rails."[31]

Hasbrouck also noted Roosevelt's sense of humor: "On yesterday afternoon—Miss Mahoney's birthday—Mr. Roosevelt . . . presented her with an old-fashioned buggy whip (tagged with a sentiment appropriate to the occasion), for use in training her performers."[32] Polio affected each patient differently so physiotherapists worked with patients during exercises to make sure they used proper muscle groups.

IN 1926, Roosevelt convinced Dr. Leroy Hubbard, formerly with the New York Board of Health, to come to Warm Springs to be chief physician. Hubbard brought Helena Mahoney along as his head physiotherapist. They had both worked with victims of the 1916 polio epidemic. At Warm Springs, they demonstrated how twenty-three patients who received treatment for five to seventeen weeks showed significant signs of improvement. Young therapists from Peabody College in Tennessee soon joined them at Warm Springs.

Roosevelt stated in 1929: "The spirit which has been inculcated into that community there through Dr. Hubbard, and the various Physio-Therapists down there, is such that the people not only swear by the place, but compete with each other, and cooperate with each other in the perfectly definite determination of getting well."[33]

As the second physiotherapist to come to Warm Springs, arriving after Mahoney, Alice Lou Plastridge accompanied Henry Pope of Chicago as he sought treatment for his daughter. Plastridge spent the next twenty-five years at the foundation, while Pope served as one of the first trustees. Plastridge lived in the old Meriwether Inn and later in one of the cottages. She remembered that Roosevelt would come to the pools, usually by 10:00 or 11:00 a.m., and exercise after he sunbathed. Exercise sessions were a serious time for Roosevelt and all the patients, but after they worked, patients and staff alike enjoyed playing in the water. After Roosevelt's death, Plastridge recalled:

> I miss him because he was lots of fun playing jokes on everybody. . . . [One day] we finally finished with the exercises . . . everyone else had gone . . . and he looked at me with a twinkle in his eye and said you want to see me play a joke on the secret service men? . . . He just dove down . . . and swam under water the width

of the pool to the lower outlet that goes into the channel that goes to the outside pool as it used to do. . . . He swam to the third pool which was our outdoor work pool and he hid under the stairs. . . . I started to get out of the pool. . . . I knew Gus had seen and would be on the job if anything happened. . . . As I started up the stairs a secret service man came to the door. . . . They looked around and they couldn't see Mr. Roosevelt and they . . . were simply frantic and they ran around like a lot of ants and . . . they said where is he . . . and finally someone spotted him way out in the outside pool. . . . I am sure he had such fun![34]

THIS PHOTOGRAPH shows Roosevelt in his 1920s swimming outfit and floppy hat, relaxing by the pool at Warm Springs. During the decade, he gained friends and fans throughout West Georgia. The *Meriwether Vindicator* declared: "He is truly great in the things that make men great. He has a brilliant mind and a big heart. . . . Mr. Roosevelt has the appearance of a great big boy, with a countenance that at once captures you with its sincerity and perpetual smile. . . . History will, in our opinion, record the fact that another Roosevelt whose given name is Franklin, was president of the United States."[35]

After he became governor of New York and later president of the United States, Roosevelt continued to swim at Warm Springs and played water sports with young patients. Several times during the Depression years of the 1930s, staff of Warm Springs Institute discussed closing the public pool as a cost-saving measure, but each time, Roosevelt spoke in favor of keeping the pool opened for the enjoyment of area residents. During his final visit in April 1945, he agreed with Basil O'Connor and Leighton McCarthy on the need to close the public pools because they did not help patients and required expensive maintenance.[36] During a special observance on the fiftieth anniversary of Roosevelt's death, a touch pool, or basin in the center pool, allowed visitors to feel the waters of Warm Springs. The pool and a new museum were opened and dedicated by an audience that included President Bill Clinton, former president Jimmy Carter, and former United Nations ambassador Andrew Young.

ON DECEMBER 3, 1929, Governor Roosevelt met with medical and science advisors of the Warm Springs Institute. Pictured from left are the chauffeur P. M. Snyder, Dr. Oskar Baudisch, Roosevelt, Dr. Paul Haertl, and Mr. Schoenborn on the porch of Roosevelt's home, now known as McCarthy Cottage. In the summer of 1927, Dr. Baudisch, a native of Austria, spent several days studying the mineral content of the water at Warm Springs. He later worked at the New York Institute at Saratoga Springs, a popular spa treatment center. Dr. Haertl was the managing director of the Bad Kissingen spa in Germany and served on the Board of Medical Consultants of Warm Springs, which included physicians from around the world. Haertl and Baudisch each traveled to Warm Springs several times to conduct scientific experiments. Extensive testing confirmed that the value of the water lay in the steady temperature and not in its mineral content.[37] Haertl's visits included the 1933 Thanksgiving dinner, when he brought books, cakes, toys, and other items from Germany as gifts for young patients at Warm Springs.

Despite medical and scientific attention, conditions remained crude throughout the 1920s. Bill Trotter later remembered: "When Warm Springs first got an x-ray machine, they had to fire up the boilers at Manchester Mills and run it through the City of Manchester's electric plant to get enough electricity to run the x-ray machines at the Foundation." Trotter's father managed the mill during that time and helped the foundation with such details.[38]

PATIENTS AND STAFF at Warm Springs gathered to celebrate Roosevelt's 1928 election as governor of New York—complete with costumes, a parade, and the old stagecoach. Built in nearby Barnesville, the stagecoach carried guests from the railroad station into town, to the inn, or to nearby White Sulphur Springs for years. With the coming of the automobile, the stagecoach appeared only on special occasions. The driver in top hat is Fred Botts, the girl on the left is Mary Hudson (later Veeder), on the right is Martha Parker (later Mays), and the clowns on horses are push boys who usually helped patients. Hudson and Parker were physiotherapists.

A native of Warm Springs, Suzanne Pike was born with clubfeet and, as a young baby, became the first nonpolio patient at the foundation. She remembered: "I got so much from the spirit of Warm Springs. . . . We didn't call it a hospital. It was a campus. It was just like a big home. . . . We made our own entertainment. We had the theater where they showed us movies twice a week if we did our homework."[39]

At Thanksgiving dinner in 1939, Roosevelt spoke of this atmosphere.

It seems to me also that here at Warm Springs we have discovered something that has not yet been recognized as a fact all over the United States, and that is . . . the relation-ship of that human relationship to science and medicine. Way back there, fifteen years . . . there came into being a thing called "the Spirit of Warm Springs." . . . I do hope to see Warm Springs go on in the position to give the spirit of Warm Springs, the human asso-ciations, the general feelings that we are all part of a family, that we are having a pretty good time out of it all, getting well not only in our legs and arms but also helping our minds in relationship to the minds of everybody around us.[40]

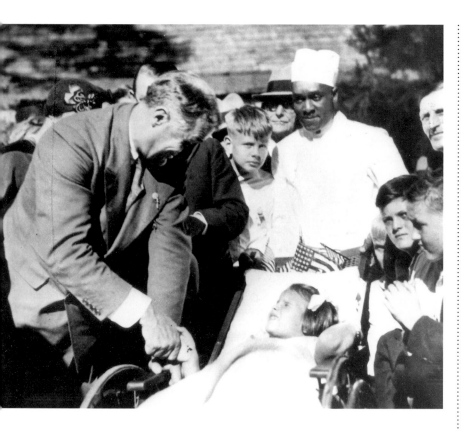

WHEN ROOSEVELT stopped in Warm Springs, he would always visit with patients and staff at the foundation, including patients in hospital beds. Children living in the Warm Springs area also often felt Roosevelt's love and concern. Flora W. Cramer remembered being a small child living in Warm Springs and seeing folks "dressed up" and passing by her home. She followed them and decided she wanted to see "Mr. Present." She ended up in a kitchen at the foundation. She screamed when she saw a chef with a meat cleaver, but the staff gave her candy, and finally Roosevelt arrived. She asked him, "Do you give presents?" He had her close her eyes, put some paper in her hand, and told her to go straight home. She skipped along, singing to herself, "Mr. President gave me a present!" When she got home, her mother discovered she had ten dollars in her hand—a tremendous sum in the mid-1930s. A couple of days passed before her mother realized that the money came from "the head of the whole country!" This realization meant that they could keep the money, part of which was used for a foot operation (Flora had twin toes on both feet), while fifty cents went to buy her a new dress. Young Flora left the area soon afterward, but years later she fondly remembered meeting her president.[41]

Warm Springs provided a place for Roosevelt to relax and get treatment and a cause to believe in that he shared with both polio victims and healthy people. He realized that if he had benefited from the warm waters and polio care, then others would also gain from the experience. Paul Rogers stated: "I think you can give a hundred percent of the credit to FDR . . . while some of us didn't agree with him politically, I think the development of the whole Foundation was his idea and it was something he didn't have to do. He could just have come down here with his own physio and doctor and done what good there was to be done."[42]

IN THE MID-1930S, Roosevelt's January 30 birthday became the focus of fund-raising efforts for the Warm Springs Foundation, a nonprofit institution. On his fifty-first birthday, patients and residents of Warm Springs greeted him with a party, complete with chocolate cake. Roosevelt became the thirty-second president of the United States five weeks later. Eleanor stands just behind him while daughter Anna Roosevelt Dall sits on his left. A lottery system determined which patients got to sit near Roosevelt at these gatherings.

The following year, birthday balls first began to put the foundation on sound financial footing. These parties raised funds for the March on Polio, which later became the March of Dimes. Thousands of towns across the United States held fund-raising events with the proceeds going to the Warm Springs Foundation. Citizens contributed over one million dollars in the campaign. For example, residents in nearby LaGrange, Georgia, held a 1934 party at the high school gym featuring an orchestra, dancing, a magician, stunts, an appearance by the Mercer Glee Club, and a broadcast from the president. An absent guest at all the parties after 1933, Roosevelt spent birthday evenings with the "cuff links gang," friends who had helped in his unsuccessful bid for the vice presidency in 1920. Following the 1934 ball, 70 percent of the monies raised stayed at polio treatment centers located near the community raising the funds, while 30 percent went to research and the center at Warm Springs.

POLIO PATIENTS relearned social skills and gained confidence as they interacted with others. In accepting a check for over $1 million from the Birthday Balls for the Georgia Warm Springs Foundation, Roosevelt outlined planned spending of the money "based on a realization of the scope of the problem created by a disease which alone account[ed] for one-third of those people, children and adults, in our country who [were] crippled from any cause other than injury in accidents." One hundred thousand dollars were set aside "to stimulate and further the meritorious work being done in the field of infantile paralysis." Roosevelt noted, "It is the present intention that this fund will be used in connection with work done elsewhere than at Warm Springs so that the greatest encouragement may be given to others interested in this problem."[43]

The widespread success of these birthday balls garnered both support and controversy. Some people felt that the president took advantage of his position to help fund his favorite cause. Eckford DeKay, an attorney in New York City, wrote the president on March 21, 1934: "My dear Frank . . . I heard a bunch on the New Canaan express discussing you this morning. . . . They insinuated that 'knowingly or unknowingly,' you would nevertheless, benefit through your ownership of property at Warm Springs GA by the expansion and extension of the wonderful sanitarium. . . . [It] would look very badly if the expansion at Warm Springs due to the Nation's gifts to you on your birthday should result in personal profit to you through a rise in values of the adjoining properties you took over from Mr. George Foster Peabody."[44]

Roosevelt responded with a strong defense of the parties. "I am not the least bit surprised at the snarling curs who would gladly crucify their own mothers if it would help their own pocketbooks. The story about Warm Springs' land is exceedingly simple. When the Foundation was started we all believed that it would be to its advantage to control the wonderful top of the mountain. . . . The Foundation had no money to acquire any of this land and, therefore, I acquired it myself and at the same time gave to the Foundation a written option to purchase it back from me at any time at exactly the price which I paid for it. . . . I have no objection to your showing this to some of the Pharisees on the New Canaan express just so long as it does not get into the papers!"[45]

After Roosevelt's death, officials at the Georgia Warm Springs Foundation and the National Foundation for Infantile Paralysis began to discourage the birthday balls, though the Roosevelt Warm Springs Rehabilitation Institute started hosting a Founder's Day Ball honoring Roosevelt's birthday decades later.

49

TRUSTEES OF THE Warm Springs Foundation gathered for a board meeting in the early 1930s. The men seated in the front row in the photograph are, from left, Dr. Leroy Hubbard, head of medical services; Roosevelt; and Leighton McCarthy. In the back are Paul G. Richter; George Foster Peabody; Basil O'Connor; Arthur Carpenter, business manager for the foundation; and Frank C. Root of Greenwich, Connecticut. The trustees met regularly, charted the development of the foundation, and assisted with fund-raising. They sought to increase the patients' aid fund, which supported those who could not afford treatment. In the fall of 1931, Dr. Hubbard began to travel to areas with polio epidemics, advise hospitals on medical treatment, and, as Roosevelt said, "spread abroad the gospel of Warm Springs that infantile paralysis can and will be conquered." The trustees encouraged this expansion of the foundation's work. They wanted to improve care for polio victims beyond Warm Springs. In November 1934, Roosevelt stated their views: "Ours, therefore, must be ever the greater aim—to maintain here the example of the right way of giving help so that throughout our land other groups and other buildings may carry the torch to the handicapped and crippled wherever they may be."[46]

Roosevelt worked hard to put Warm Springs on solid financial footing, so he generally sought wealthy businessmen with strong Wall Street ties to fill seats on the foundation's board of trustees. Georgians and southerners remained somewhat absent from both the early boards and Roosevelt's "Brain Trust," the group that helped establish policies during the New Deal days of his presidency. Peabody, a banker, philanthropist, and native of Columbus who resided in New York State; Cason Callaway, businessman and textile manufacturer; and Richard B. Russell Jr., governor and later U.S. senator, were notable exceptions. Roosevelt loved Georgians and enjoyed talking to residents of the state, but southerners usually did not become his closest confidants and advisors.[47]

BASIL O'CONNOR stands with Roosevelt, his law partner, in front of McCarthy Cottage at Warm Springs, probably in December 1928, just after the New York gubernatorial election. Roosevelt chose his partner to head the Georgia Warm Springs Foundation. In September 1937, O'Connor joined the National Foundation for Infantile Paralysis to lead the fight against polio. He often accompanied Roosevelt on his trips to Warm Springs.

Roosevelt described O'Connor at the foundation's annual Thanksgiving dinner on November 30, 1933:

> I was very fortunate in those past years in having as my law partner a man who is not only a good lawyer, and, believe me, they are mighty rare, but also a man who understood what this work was all about, and who has given unselfishly and without pay—which is something that most lawyers don't do—a great deal of time and effort in keeping our books straight and proving to the public that we were a sound financial institution. More than that, he has given of his time and his influence and his money in showing the city of New York and the United States something about the ideals that we all have.[48]

BY THE FALL OF 1933, Roosevelt had given the nation a shot of confidence to face the Great Depression, and he now returned triumphantly to Warm Springs for the opening of Georgia Hall. This administrative building and cafeteria opened during his first visit as president of the United States. The idea for the building developed during discussions between Cason Callaway and Cator Woolford, an Atlanta businessman who helped found Retail Credit Company (now Equifax). They wanted a way for Georgians to show their appreciation to the new president. One photograph captured Roosevelt seated at the head table and carving a turkey. Leighton McCarthy watched at Roosevelt's left; at his right sat Basil O'Connor, with Callaway beside him and Woolford on the far right. Patients watched from the surrounding

campaign fund. Governor-elect Eugene Talmadge, who served as county campaign chair of the Georgia Hall campaign, acted as auctioneer at the Healey Building in Atlanta, while Mrs. Healey stood with the cotton bale. This fundraising effort marked the first time that Warm Springs had attracted the interest and support of the general population.

Arthur Carpenter, resident trustee of the foundation, had commented earlier that year: "This cornerstone laying is more than a cornerstone laying of Georgia Hall, it is a cornerstone laying of the Foundation. . . . The realization of an unselfish dream had by one man, Franklin D. Roosevelt, who heads this institution and the man who at present heads the United States."[49] The building featured wide doorways, rubberized floor coverings for ease when walking with crutches, a lower lobby desk, and restrooms designed for use by people in wheelchairs.

Roosevelt thanked Georgians for their gift and dedicated its use to the patients of Warm Springs. "You have made me very happy tonight. You have contributed to the great ideal of humanity a service of distinction both to your state and to your nation." He talked about the work of the Warm Springs Foundation. "Every social objective requires that the child be rehabilitated to lead a normal life—to become a useful member of society. In accomplishing this we reach at the same time, the economic objective . . . and enable that person to be an economically useful unit in the community." He concluded by assuring the audience that he wished people all over the country could be there "to see this beautiful building which for all time will be the center of our work, and especially to understand that thing which we call 'the spirit of Warm Springs' which does so much to supplement the skill of science."[50]

tables. In another photograph, Roosevelt stood with his arm through his son Franklin Jr.'s arm; with them were Woolford (second from left), Callaway (next to FDR), and George F. Peabody (right). The Emory University Glee Club provided musical entertainment for the evening.

Fifty thousand state residents contributed $125,000 to build Georgia Hall. Batson-Cook of West Point, Georgia, constructed the building. As chair of the Georgia Hall Committee, Cason Callaway made one of the first contributions to the fund when he purchased and then sold the first bale of cotton placed on the Georgia market in 1932. Both times, he added $700 to the funds for the Warm Springs Foundation. L. W. "Chip" Robert had originally purchased the bale in July and then turned it over to Mrs. William Healey to be disposed of to benefit the national Democratic

VISITORS DURING the two weeks of the president's stay included Mr. and Mrs. John R. Marsh. Marsh handled public relations for Georgia Power, while Mrs. Marsh gained fame three years later, when she used her maiden name, Margaret Mitchell, as the author of *Gone with the Wind*. J. M. Schenck, president of United Arts Corporation, also visited the foundation during that trip.

Roosevelt participated in the design of several buildings at Warm Springs. Architect Henry Toombs and business manager Arthur Carpenter evidently worried that then-candidate Roosevelt would get involved in the design of Georgia Hall. Toombs recalled: "When plans for Georgia Hall were under consideration . . . we only showed Governor Roosevelt a simple single-line drawing, having agreed between ourselves that if we showed him the detail drawings, he would surely be full of ideas and probably upset our plans, which were already far along. We had noted that when F.D.R. saw a drawing he always reached for a pencil."[51]

The Meriwether Inn stood just behind Georgia Hall. A plaque now marks the spot where the inn stood.

IN 1926, Roosevelt established the annual Founder's Day dinners as a time to remember and honor the early days of the polio center. Thirty-five guests attended. Nine years later, four hundred guests joined the first family in devouring fourteen turkeys, including ones sent from Salt Lake City, Utah, and Brady, Texas. An elegantly dressed Eleanor Roosevelt watched her husband carve turkey surrounded by thirteen boys and girls. The menu consisted of turkey, hearts of celery, olives, toasted Georgia pecans, cranberry sauce, gravy, sage stuffing, creamed potato balls, English peas, julienne carrots, salad, rolls, plum pudding, and pumpkin pies.

Mary Marshal Neir described one of the dinners. "Mr. Roosevelt said the Thanksgiving prayer. They brought a beautiful big, big turkey in from the kitchen. . . . He started carving it . . . All the time, he was talking to the patients . . . just like a father would talk to his family. That's the way he treated them all, like a family."[52] Suzanne Pike remembered being asked to sit at the president's table after she first learned to

stand with braces and crutches. "I really didn't want to go but my mother said 'you're not invited every day to go to Thanksgiving dinner with the President and you do want to go' so I did go and I met him. He was at Georgia Hall and he greeted every patient who came through the hall. If he'd ever met you, he would always know your name." She remembered meeting him. "When I rolled up to Georgia Hall in my wooden wheelchair, I looked up at him and I thought he was the tallest man I'd ever seen. . . . The small children called him Rosie, the older children called him Doc Roosevelt. . . . He gave us so much strength to go on." Whenever these patients came up against something that was hard to do, such as going down steps with braces, they knew that he had faced similar hurdles.[53]

Roosevelt also celebrated a family Thanksgiving with whoever happened to be at Warm Springs. In 1935, he, Eleanor, and son James had a private dinner at the Little White House earlier in the day. Though Eleanor did not often dress up, special occasions at Warm Springs called for the finest clothes. Franklin Roosevelt once talked with Frances Perkins about how lovely his wife looked. "She always looks magnificent in evening clothes, doesn't she?"[54]

Eleanor later reflected on these Thanksgiving celebrations: "For a number of years, my husband went to Warm Springs every autumn, and I remember with a mixture of joy and sadness the Thanksgiving Day celebrations. There seemed so much happiness in the children's faces, but the complete gallantry of all the patients always brought a choke to my throat. . . . Some hoped to get well, many faced permanent handicaps, but all were cheerful that one evening at least."[55]

Thanksgiving celebrations often included visitors from across the South and the nation. In addition to political leaders, members of social and civic groups would participate. Women's clubs from around Georgia often decorated the dining room for the Thanksgiving meal. In 1933, the Woman's Club of Waycross (located over two hundred miles away) decorated tables and told the president how anxious they were to have a canal dredged across the Okefenokee Swamp connecting the St. Mary's and the Suwanee Rivers to open a channel to the Atlantic Ocean for commerce. They brought a display featuring a miniature swamp with a canal. After dinner, politics, polio, and all else were forgotten as musicians, including groups such as the Morehouse Male Quartet, played and Roosevelt spoke, often reflecting on the history of the foundation.[56] The agenda for this dinner included "7:05–7:20 Photos—sound pictures. Photographers have requested that the President carve turkey and talk to small children. This will be just for photographers and serving of dinner will be delayed until it is complete."[57]

WITH THE AID OF assistants, family members, and the press, Roosevelt hid his paralysis from the public even while working to improve treatment for those stricken with polio. Even when showing Roosevelt talking with polio patients, reporters did not photograph him in his wheelchair. This group photograph in the dining room of Georgia Hall clearly represents what author Hugh Gallagher calls "a splendid deception." On April 1, 1938, Eleanor and Franklin gathered with Jane Daly, of Spring Valley, New York; Jerry Gould, of Scranton, Pennsylvania (center); and Jack Burney, of Columbus, Georgia. During a luncheon that day, Roosevelt announced that a new thirty-five-bed hospital would be built

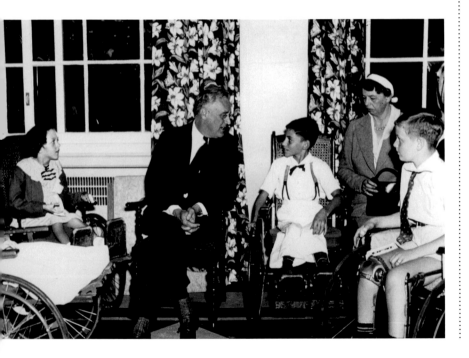

at the foundation. The hospital would have space for surgeries, thus saving patients from having to travel to Atlanta. In his relaxed speaking style, he told the audience, "It is going to be pretty noisy—going to be noisier than Jerry," referring to Scranton and the new construction.[58]

Judge Frank Cheatham remembered his first Thanksgiving dinner at Warm Springs in the early 1930s when he was nine. After dinner, "the President laboriously got out of his wheelchair. After he was standing, he backed up against the door frame. . . . Then he shook hands with everyone there, the President was sending a silent message to the patients in the room: Look at me, you see my handicap, I am president of the United States, the most powerful nation in the world. If I can be president with this handicap, then you can be anything you want to be."[59]

Editors of the *Meriwether Vindicator* presented another perspective on Roosevelt's visits. "The president is a lonely man. He enjoys associating with people, nothing he loves better. But he must wear the cross alone. He loves to come to Warm Springs. He lives there next to nature. He loves those afflicted as he. They are his pets. Never happier than when among them."[60]

WITH NAVAL OFFICERS in the back seat, Roosevelt shakes hands with a polio patient. The door on the brick building behind the car reads "Navy Polio Office." Samuel H., Rush H., and Claude W. Kress donated most of the funds for Kress Hall, which was built in 1934 as housing for foundation patients. The U.S. Navy used Kress during the 1930s and World War II to treat sailors afflicted with polio. Roosevelt set an example for thousands of victims of polio. Later, during World War II, he became a symbol of conquering adversity for injured soldiers.

Visits from leaders in government, the military, and business naturally put the spotlight on Warm Springs. Foundation leaders worked hard to ensure that medical and therapeutic care continued as usual. Arthur Carpenter wrote presidential secretary Steve Early in November 1937 to express his concerns about the many visitors. He stressed the need to avoid overemphasizing social activity, overcrowding the facility with too many guests, and thus giving a false impression about the purpose of the foundation.[61]

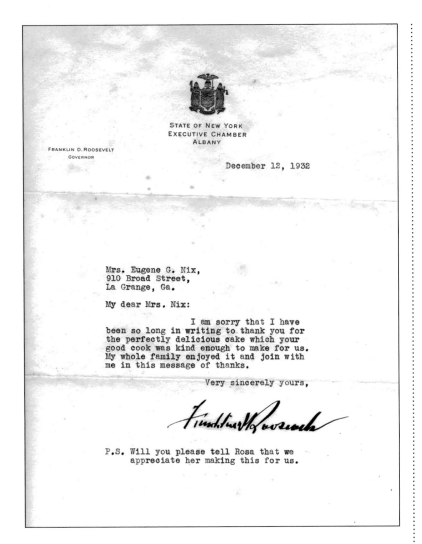

STATE OF NEW YORK
EXECUTIVE CHAMBER
ALBANY

FRANKLIN D. ROOSEVELT
GOVERNOR

December 12, 1932

Mrs. Eugene G. Nix,
910 Broad Street,
La Grange, Ga.

My dear Mrs. Nix:

  I am sorry that I have
been so long in writing to thank you for
the perfectly delicious cake which your
good cook was kind enough to make for us.
My whole family enjoyed it and join with
me in this message of thanks.

    Very sincerely yours,

Franklin D. Roosevelt

P.S. Will you please tell Rosa that we
appreciate her making this for us.

THE PEOPLE OF GEORGIA loved to shower their New York neighbor with gifts. They brought him jams, desserts, hams, chickens, walking canes, and more. (Many of these walking sticks remain on display at the Little White House museum today.) Eugenia Gay Nix and her daughters, Mary, Julia, and Carrie, supported Roosevelt. They saved this thank-you letter even though the president-elect did not quite get their mother's name right. Eleanor Roosevelt once commented that these gifts of food delighted her husband, and he ate them with more enthusiasm than he normally did with food at the White House, which was often fairly tasteless and routine.[62]

Barbara Rossmore of Upper Montclair, New Jersey, remembered: "I knew Eleanor Roosevelt when I was a child with polio down at Warm Springs, Georgia. . . . She often had a reception for the local farm women who came in in poke bonnets and heavy men's work shoes; they walked all the way from their homes many miles away. They brought presents of the only things they had . . . and Mrs. Roosevelt carefully wrote each individual name and FDR on the label. Months later the farm women would proudly show around notes from the White House. . . . I was about ten years old then, but even now, some thirty years later, I still remember the great love we all had for Eleanor Roosevelt!"[63]

Mr. and Mrs. Lee Rowe remembered providing Roosevelt with eggs, butter, and other produce during his early visits at Warm Springs. When Rexford Tugwell asked if they took the chickens alive or dressed, Mrs. Rowe replied: "He always got them alive. He always came to get his chickens when he wanted them. . . . Mr. Roosevelt liked fresh meat alright. He liked pigs' feet always on Thanksgiving. . . . We always killed hogs on Thanksgiving and I would go up there and take him fresh meat."[64] Daisy Bonner, his longtime Warm Springs cook, would prepare the pigs feet.

FROM THE EARLY 1930S until Roosevelt's death in 1945, Daisy Bonner cooked for him each time he came to Warm Springs. During the president's absence, she cooked at other cottages, including for the Fryer and the Glenn families. Mrs. Livingston Fryer offered Bonner's services to the president for his March 1945 trip to Georgia. Bonner told Rexford Tugwell: "He would eat anything I fixed for him. I had him eating corn bread and turnip greens." Other favorites included Country Captain, turkey and stuffing, and cheese and lamb soufflés. Most of his meals were eaten with no more than four or five people. Bonner gained the affection of later visitors to the Little White House when she wrote on the chalkboard in the kitchen, "Daisy Bonner, cooked the first and last meal in the Little White House." She recalled: "That handwriting on the wall . . . I thought of that many times since the President passed. Why did I write that on the wall? Why I did that I don't know."[65]

Bonner recounted how one particular night she had problems getting in the Little White House. She had left the grounds with one team of Secret Service agents in charge and came back later. A different team of agents would not let her into the house, and she spent the night at the foundation playing cards. Finally, the next morning after the president had breakfast, someone saw Bonner and said:

> Come on and let's take it to the President and he carried me in [to the Little White House]. That was the first time I went through the front door—of course I was shaking so much. I didn't know what was going to happen. We went in and addressed the President like they addressed him. I was so sick, I was scared to address him any kind of way—I didn't know what he was going to say because I didn't give him his breakfast— and he started laughing and he said, well, well, the Marines were on the dock—and he never did say anything to me and so that was quite a joke and I said well, sir, the President doesn't take nothing hard.[66]

GEORGIA WILKINS, ministers, and others met with the president on Sunday, March 27, 1938, to dedicate the new chapel at the Warm Springs Foundation. Her uncle Charles L. Davis owned the Meriwether Inn for many years, and Wilkins sold land at Warm Springs to Roosevelt. She contributed funds to build the chapel in memory of her great-grandparents, John and Julia Mustian, one-time owners of the land. (The Mustian home became the museum on the grounds of the Little White House in 1961.) Architect Henry Toombs designed the nondenominational chapel with wide rows and aisles for patients in wheel chairs. Second from left is Rev. J. D. Wilson of St. Mark's Episcopal Church in LaGrange. On his left are William C. Bullitt, U.S. ambassador to France; Georgia Wilkins; Bishop Henry J. Mikell of the Episcopal Diocese of Atlanta; and Roosevelt. Reverend Wilson had previously conducted services for patients in the small hall used as a motion picture theater. Bishop Mikell conducted the dedicatory services. Roosevelt wrote Georgia Wilkins the following week: "I did not get a chance adequately to tell you how perfectly thrilled I am by the chapel. It is lovely in every way and we are deeply grateful to you who made it possible, not only for us but for the generations to come."[67] Roosevelt attended his final church service there five days before he died.

Roosevelt introduced Georgia Wilkins to the audience at the 1933 Thanksgiving dinner at the Foundation by recalling his first visit. "All of the good people down in the Village were most kind and gave us every kind of hospitality. But outside of old Tom Lawley [*sic*], there wasn't anybody up here on the old hill except the old postmaster, but all of a sudden, one afternoon, there came up to my cottage a very charming lady, and she said, 'I am the owner of this property, or rather, I was the owner up to a short time ago.' We are happy in having the interest of the Davis family and the Wilkins family."[68]

ON APRIL 1, 1939, Roosevelt waited to give a speech at the dedication of the school at the Warm Springs Foundation. Roosevelt and the staff wanted young students to continue their studies while recuperating from surgery and treatment. Basil O'Connor holds the car door open while Elizabeth Whitehead Pierson sits in the back. Her father, James Whitehead of Detroit, served as a foundation trustee. His company, Whitehead and Kales, manufactured structural steel. Mrs. Pierson suffered from polio and had been a patient at Warm Springs in the 1920s and 1930s. She spoke at the dedication on behalf of Katherine Tuck, who donated money for the school. Originally from Detroit, Mrs. Tuck gave funds for the school after being assured by William Bullitt, U.S. ambassador to France, that the school at Warm Springs was well organized and permanent, and the president would continue to be involved in its operations. Marion Huntington, a teacher at the school, is leaning against the car. Originally from New York State, Mrs. Huntington came to Warm Springs when her brother, Maurice Finney, developed polio and sought treatment. Classes had previously been held at the playhouse and in various rooms around campus. The reflection in the shiny car door reveals that a large group of people had gathered for the occasion. Roosevelt also dedicated new medical buildings that day.

Schools in Georgia are credited with being a significant influence on one post–World War II policy: the GI Bill of Rights. According to speechwriter and later advisor Samuel Rosenman, Roosevelt drafted a message to Congress in August 1943 stating: "This is a good time not merely to be thinking about the subject, but actually to do something about it. Nothing will be more conducive to the maintenance of high morale in our troops than the knowledge that steps are being taken now to give them education and training when the fighting is over." Rosenman credited conditions in the South with being one of the president's motivations. He knew Roosevelt had worried about the education children in poor areas of the country received. The president feared that some states would be unwilling or unable to improve education in poor districts. "He felt that the only way to equalize educational opportunities was through the resources and Treasury of the United States."[69]

THE PRESIDENT'S CAR pulls up in front of the Warm Springs Community House, where members of the State Women's Federated Clubs had gathered. Constructed with funds from the Works Progress Administration, one of the New Deal relief agencies, the building honored Sara Delano Roosevelt, the president's mother. Stones used in the exterior walls reflect styles more common in the Hudson Valley than in Meriwether County. The building included an auditorium plus space for city offices, a jail, and fire equipment. Roosevelt presided over a service at the new building on March 18, 1937, and then spoke at the official dedication on November 24, 1939. Despite cool weather, he chose to ride in the open air of his favorite convertible.

Mrs. R. M. Fowler, operator of the bus station at Warm Springs, later recalled the day when city officials dedicated the community house. Secret Service men gathered around him and tried to keep space between him and the crowd. He asked them to move, assuring them that those gathered were all his friends.[70]

Rev. W. G. Harry later recalled a passing remark he made as mayor at the dedication, that no one in the group would oppose Roosevelt if he chose to run for a third term. The remark got a good laugh though the president encouraged residents to ask the United States for a new post office while he still had influence in Washington. (Congress later passed a bill giving a new post office to Warm Springs; Roosevelt vetoed it when projects he opposed were added.)[71]

A VALET helps Roosevelt out of his car at Warm Springs. Though driving and riding in cars allowed him great freedom of movement, he needed assistance entering and leaving automobiles. He had mechanics adapt his cars so that he could drive using a system of ropes and pulleys to operate the clutch, brakes, and gas. He usually had African American aides who helped him with cars and with more basic things in life, such as getting dressed in the morning. A kind man, Roosevelt often helped them in times of need. Mary Williams cooked for the New Yorker during most of his visits in the 1920s and early 1930s. When she fell ill in 1934, her daughter Jessie Lou Henderson wrote the president a note. He visited their home in Manchester and gave her a donation. She remembered, "I was flat broke that day. . . . I used some of the money to bury her" when she died a few days later.[72]

BASIL O'CONNOR, president of the National Foundation for Infantile Paralysis, announced a grant of $161,350 to establish a center to fight polio in nearby Tuskegee, Alabama. According to the *Warm Springs Mirror* on May 26, 1939, "funds would be used to build, equip and maintain for a year a center of 36 beds to train Negro doctors, surgeons and nurses in the effort to control infantile paralysis among Negroes." Roosevelt, together with leaders at Warm Springs and the National Foundation, had opted for separate facilities for the races as they fought against polio. Warm Springs could treat about 150 patients. The whites-only policy at Warm Springs had begun to cause political problems for Roosevelt. Complaints about even the poorest of white children being able to get treatment at Warm Springs but all blacks being turned away began to appear occasionally in the prominent newspapers. Occasionally, even white children who did not have polio received treatment at Warm Springs, yet African Americans with polio had to go elsewhere. Within a decade, black patients began to be treated on a limited basis at Warm Springs.[73]

CHAPTER 3

An Active Man

BETWEEN 1924 AND 1928, Roosevelt made numerous appearances in west and middle Georgia. He talked to Sunday school classes (including those at Bullochville Baptist and First Methodist of Greenville), addressed civic groups, and met with local leaders. The Ku Klux Klan had been intensively active in 1924 in the South and elsewhere. Roosevelt first got involved in Georgia state politics when he sent a telegram to the *Atlanta Constitution* rebutting charges made by Georgia governor Clifford Walker at the National KKK Klonvocation in Kansas City. Walker had joined the Klan and consulted with it on issues. Roosevelt denied one of his statements and said that President Woodrow Wilson had not shown preferences to the Catholic Church or any creed or religion during World War I. Writing as one who had served in Wilson's administration, Roosevelt acknowledged: "It is perhaps not in the part of courtesy for me as a visitor in this state and as the recipient of the generous hospitality of your citizens to comment on the propriety of your governor making this speech at all." He added that he knew that Georgia citizens and citizens of the entire United States regretted the actions of the governor.[1]

Ironically, one of Clifford Walker's few accomplishments as governor of Georgia was creating the Georgia Forestry Commission, a move that Roosevelt surely appreciated since he thought Georgians should grow more trees.[2]

Also during his first visit, local residents celebrated the merger of the towns of Bullochville and Warm Springs. Ironically, Roosevelt joined them as an honored guest on the occasion when the two towns became one city and the Bullochville name, which shared the last name of Mittie Bulloch, Roosevelt's great-grandmother, became part of history. The towns had both incorporated in 1893, one on the east side of the Southern Railway tracks and the other on the west.[3]

In 1928, Roosevelt's activities when he was at Warm Springs began to change. He took up horseback riding and fishing and began making more speeches in Georgia. Mary Veeder, a physiotherapist, reported that he spent hours learning to walk using someone's elbow so that he appeared to be walking on his own. Here he mounted a dark mare for a ride near his cottage at Warm Springs in 1930. He rides with Ed Flynn, a fellow New Yorker. Photos such as this one appeared only during this "active man" campaign.

DURING HIS STAYS at Warm Springs in the 1920s, Roosevelt spoke mostly in nearby cities. In February 1928, he motored south to Americus to speak to members of the chamber of commerce at their annual meeting. Walter Rylander and Harvey Mathis, representing the chamber, traveled to Warm Springs and accompanied Roosevelt and his party back to Americus. Held at the Windsor Hotel (shown in the photograph), the event attracted 208 people, including, as front page headlines in the *Americus Times-Recorder* noted, "More than 50 Women." The newspaper touted Roosevelt as "one of the outstanding possible Democratic nominees for the presidency at Houston in July of this year."[4]

The evening featured musical presentations by the American Legion band and the "Americus negro quartet," which "not only delighted Mr. Roosevelt, but all the guests, with the negro spirituals sung by them." Earlier, the paper reported that the quartet had been "secured for the pleasure of Mr. Roosevelt and at his request." In his address, Roosevelt called those gathered neighbors and stated: "Americus has sold itself to me in the short time I have been here. . . . I wish I could get around your great state more than I have. This I would do but for your roads." He gave more compliments when talking about the people of the state. "You are blossoming out with the new spirit of progress which for a long time lay dormant. . . . I would rather tackle new things in Georgia than attempt to rehash things in New York. You are young in spirit and are not handicapped as we are up there."[5] Despite criticizing his home state, however, he agreed to run for governor of New York eight months later.

He then talked about one of his favorite topics, trees and the need to reforest the countryside. He thought trees could become a major cash crop for his adopted state. "No American should be asked to farm lands like some of those which I passed through today. . . . These are fair lands which should be reforested and in time will bring the owner great wealth."[6]

BEFORE HE CONTRACTED POLIO, Roosevelt enjoyed golf. Afterward, he never took up the sport but made sure that Warm Springs had a golf course, perhaps part of his desire to have activities for wealthy guests. He also knew that appearing at a golf course with golfers would further his effort to appear physically fit. A nine-hole course was built with expectations of increasing the size to eighteen holes. Though the expansion never came, golfers continue to play on the Donald Ross–designed course.

In this October 1931 photograph, Roosevelt chats with golfers at Warm Springs. The men are, from left, Warren Mays, Warm Springs professional; Fred Haskins, Columbus pro; Charles R. Yates, amateur champion of Atlanta and Georgia; and John H. Ridley of LaGrange and Atlanta. Several of Roosevelt's sons golfed at the course over the years.

Following a visit to LaGrange in March 1927, Roosevelt told editors of the *LaGrange Reporter*, "Speaking of golf, I am a strong believer in reciprocity, and I want to take this opportunity to invite Mr. Cason Callaway [a textile manufacturer] and other LaGrange golfers who have been so kind to us Warm Springs folk to come over and enjoy our course as soon as it is in shape."[7]

ROOSEVELT CHECKED on a herd of cattle and crops while out on drives. In October 1932, he visited with Wes Anderson, C. M. Camp, Otis Moore, Basil O'Connor in the back seat, and Ed Doyle, with Atlantan A. L. Belle Isle in the driver's seat. Despite the casual appearance, the Georgia farm scene seems to have been carefully staged. Residents of Warm Springs recount stories of moving scrawny cows away from roadside fields when they expected Roosevelt to be driving by since they wanted him to see only fat cows![8]

Moore supervised Roosevelt's farming operations in the 1930s. Ed Doyle originally owned a farm on Pine Mountain and managed Roosevelt's farm from the late 1920s until 1933. After being elected president, Roosevelt appointed Doyle as U.S. Marshall in Middle Georgia, partially as repayment for watching over his farm in the 1920s. During the Depression years, the government salary assured Doyle of both a steady salary and money for college educations for his children. Another photo captured Roosevelt talking to two of the men.

Throughout his years in Georgia, Roosevelt sought to improve the economies of his farm and others in the South. He often told the story about an early trip when he was awakened at the same time every night by a train traveling through Warm Springs. Upon discovering that the train carried milk from Wisconsin to southern consumers, he began to encourage raising dairy and beef cattle on depleted cotton lands.[9] James Roosevelt recalled trips in and around Warm Springs with his father: "I can remember going with him around visiting other farmers and his talking to them about what they got for their crops and how many acres they planted for that particular year. And I think that he began to feel that he had come very close to the agricultural picture."[10] After several years of encouraging more planting, Roosevelt over time became convinced that greater profits lay with cattle farming.

In a 1950 interview conducted by the Franklin D. Roosevelt Warm Springs Memorial Commission, W. Tap Bennett and Otis Moore recalled that Roosevelt's "aim in owning a farm near the Foundation was simply to show local farmers that any ordinary farm could be made profitable without great capital investments, provided the land was basically good and the farmer preserved the land." Bennett oversaw the nearby Pine Mountain Valley settlement. Clark Howell reported that Roosevelt became the first active member of the Georgia Beef Cattle Raisers Association organized in 1933. With the exception of registered bulls, Roosevelt never bought expensive cattle. He insisted that his bulls be available to service the neighbors' cows at no charge. By breeding native strains with blooded bulls, Roosevelt wanted to demonstrate that cattle herds could be improved and would give farmers greater options on how to use their land. Though the Roosevelt farm seldom made a profit, he succeeded in encouraging farmers in Georgia to raise cattle. He also encouraged the cultivation of grapes and peaches, both of which were grown on his farm in the 1930s.[11]

MID-SEPTEMBER 1928 marked yet another turning point in the political career of Franklin Roosevelt. He left New York for Georgia despite being pressured to run for governor. He felt the timing was wrong for Democrats and worried that his physical progress would be slowed by the demands of the office. Instead, he made speeches for fellow New Yorker Al Smith, the Democratic candidate for president of the United States. Seven thousand enthusiastic citizens greeted Roosevelt at Atlanta Municipal Auditorium on September 26. The *Atlanta Constitution* declared: "It was like the old-time days in Georgia when political campaigns inflamed the enthusiasm of virtually the entire population."[12]

Roosevelt criticized Smith's detractors for claiming they opposed his anti-Prohibition stance when in reality they did not want a Catholic as president. Roosevelt told the crowd that these people allowed their prejudices to rule their lives. He hoped that better schools would lessen their numbers. He also scoffed at Republican claims of prosperity by pointing out that much of the country was suffering economically, including "Meriwether County, Georgia, or any other part of the south where we grow cotton and peaches." After he finished, the crowd chanted their desire to hear from former governor Thomas W. Hardwick. He proceeded to denounce Herbert Hoover, the Republican nominee for president, who had the support of leading African Americans in Georgia.[13]

Roosevelt updated Eleanor and his mother with letters in late September saying he would be giving a big speech in Columbus on Thursday after having spoken recently in Atlanta. He knew that large amounts of propaganda circulated throughout the South. Nonetheless, he expected Smith to carry the southern states. He added, "I only hope they don't try to stampede the Convention tomorrow and nominate me and then adjourn!"[14]

On October 2, after he had given a speech in Manchester, Georgia, Roosevelt talked to Democratic leaders in New York State and finally allowed his name to be submitted to the Democratic convention. Roosevelt sent a telegram to Oliver Cabana, chair of the State Democratic Convention of New York: "Please give the convention this message. Every personal and family consideration has been and is against my becoming the candidate of the convention but if by accepting I can help the splendid cause of our beloved governor I will yield to your judgment."[15]

In addition to health concerns and his fear that 1928 might not be the year for the Democrats, Roosevelt hesitated to run for governor because of his heavy financial commitments at Warm Springs. John J. Raskob, a wealthy businessman who had recently been named chair of the National Democratic Committee, talked to Roosevelt on the phone on October 2. Following their discussion of Roosevelt's obligations to Warm Springs, Raskob wrote a check for $250,000. When Roosevelt refused the check, Raskob formed a committee to raise the funds while contributing $50,000 to the cause. Following that telephone conversation, Roosevelt agreed to run for governor. John T. Flynn later alleged that Roosevelt did not agree to run until Raskob had guaranteed the funds to get him out of debt at Warm Springs. Raskob countered that he gave the money because he believed in Al Smith, wanted to end Prohibition, and thought Roosevelt would help get Smith elected.

On October 4, two days after being named the Democratic nominee for governor of New York, Roosevelt appeared at the Springer Opera House in Columbus. The gathering celebrated the one hundredth anniversary of the founding of the city. The *Columbus Enquirer* described the evening as one of "the greatest political gatherings ever assembled in Columbus." Introduced as "the courageous cavalier of Democracy," Roosevelt lashed out against those who opposed Alfred E. Smith because of religion. His talk was frequently interrupted by the audience from Columbus, Fort Benning, Phenix City, and surrounding areas of Georgia and Alabama that had packed the theater, with at least 250 people listening outside on amplifiers. Roosevelt assured them that "no matter what may happen on November 6, [he was] going to keep coming back to Georgia."[16]

Those gathered in this photograph include, on left, Jack Ellis, then a group representative from Opelika, Alabama. Those in the center include Roosevelt, Walker R. Flournoy, William de L. Worsley, Mrs. Perry Burrus, Mr. and Mrs. Bentley H. Chappell, Leighton MacPherson, Henrietta Worsley, Mrs. William de L. Worsley, and Mrs. William Hart.[17]

IN NOVEMBER 1928, Roosevelt returned to Warm Springs, having won election as governor of New York by a narrow margin. He had taken a major step in showing that paralysis would not impede his ability to reach his longtime goal of becoming president of the United States. His cousin Theodore Roosevelt had set a powerful personal example earlier in the century by becoming the twenty-sixth president. The older Roosevelt served as a New York State legislator, assistant secretary of the Navy, governor of New York, vice president of the United States, and then president. By the 1920s, Franklin had already served as assistant secretary of the Navy and as a New York legislator. Being governor of the populous state of New York made him an early favorite for the 1932 or 1936 Democratic nomination for president. The decision to run for election made by Roosevelt in Georgia in 1928 proved to be one of the most significant in his political career. He had already been a losing vice-presidential candidate, and had he lost in what turned out to be a "Republican" year nationally, he might have been forgotten by the electorate. Shown with Roosevelt in this photo are Roosevelt's business partner, Basil O'Connor (far right) and Leighton McCarthy and an aide.

A CROWD estimated at over one thousand met Roosevelt's train when he arrived in Warm Springs on November 8, 1928. The *Meriwether Vindicator* stated: "We are glad that he is among us; we hope he will stay just as long as he can do so and that rest and health may be the portion which Meriwether awards him."[18]

According to Samuel Rosenman, "the fatigue of the campaign was all gone; [Roosevelt] was buoyant in spirit and mind, enthusiastic over the prospect of the Governorship."[19] During his stay, several dignitaries visited the governor-elect, including Atlanta mayor I. N. Ragsdale and Herbert H. Lehman, lieutenant governor–elect of New York. Missy LeHand also joined the group. Many discussions centered on state finances and the possibility of reducing the direct property tax. Roosevelt pointed out to reporters "that he would be absent from the state on occasion and that the experience of Col. Lehman who would be acting Governor would prove of great value." They all realized that they had a tough battle ahead since Republicans controlled the legislature. One visitor, former state senator Harvey Ferris of Utica, told Roosevelt that he intended to raise ten thousand dollars for the erection of a new structure at Warm Springs, to be called Oneida Cottage.[20]

The visitors felt enthusiastic about both the short-term and the long-term future. At a picnic at Chipley (now Pine Mountain), a speaker referred to Warm Springs as the "Summer White House after 1932."[21] In this photograph a group including Canadian businessman Leighton McCarthy (to the right of Roosevelt) and Roosevelt's law partner and president of the Georgia Warm Springs Foundation Basil O'Conner (in the middle right), gather beside an automobile parked near one of the Warm Springs cottages.

ROOSEVELT TRAVELED northwest from Warm Springs on May 8, 1929, to address the graduating class of the Fourth District Agricultural & Mechanical College in Carrollton (shown in the photograph; now the University of West Georgia). His speech focused on a common theme in his Georgia talks: the need to improve farm life and agriculture. He declared that several things must change before "the agricultural population [might] keep pace with the tremendous strides of present day civilization." He thought that teaching home economics both at schools like A & M and in elementary and high schools would begin to improve home conditions. He declared, "Georgia may well be proud of her work along these lines; but this work needs expansion."[22]

Roosevelt insisted that agricultural methods needed to be improved, and he blamed farm failures on the "lack of capital available for scientific farming." A third problem lay in "local government inefficiency. Local taxes [were] unnecessarily high and [were] wastefully used in almost every rural county in America." His recommended solutions included "a greater interest in the part of the average man and woman citizen in the conduct of . . . local government" and a statewide point of view with cooperation between counties. He concluded by recognizing the graduates: "This generation has educational advantages undreamed of by their fathers and mothers. The responsibility will soon rest in their hands . . . in that lies the hope of the future."[23]

Editors of the *Carroll County Times* declared: "Governor Roosevelt came, saw, and conquered Carrollton on his visit, Wednesday. He possesses a most charming personality, has the famous Roosevelt smile and he impresses one at once with his sincerity and friendliness." Rain caused graduation exercises to be moved from the A & M campus to Tabernacle Baptist Church in Carrollton. The mayor had urged businesses to close that morning, and a large crowd attended. After the address, Roosevelt shook hands with all fifty-seven young men and women who were members of the senior class. The paper added: "The Governor possesses a characteristic that many great men do not have and that is the ability to unbend. He is a most human person and wins one on first acquaintance."[24] After the ceremonies, the local Civitan Club gave a barbecue in his honor. He returned to Warm Springs accompanied by his friend Judge Henry Revill of Greenville.

PUBLIC SQUARE, PARTIAL VIEW, CARROLLTON, GA.

IN THE SPRING OF 1929 Roosevelt, Missy LeHand, and Mrs. Basil O'Connor stood amid Georgia pine trees. As Roosevelt leans against his car, the three are perhaps trying to repair glasses held by LeHand. At the time, Roosevelt had been governor of the State of New York for only a few months. To the surprise of some, he had stayed in New York throughout the legislative session though he spent much of that time fighting with lawmakers.

Missy LeHand accompanied Roosevelt on almost all of his trips to Warm Springs from 1924 to 1941. Institute staff, patients, and area residents knew and liked her. The *Meriwether Vindicator* offered this description of her on December 6, 1935: "Perhaps she knows him better than anyone other than his wife. She is a handsome young woman, yea, pretty, with a rare charm of manner which is at once attractive. She is the president's almost constant companion, and unlike the proverbial woman, does keep secrets. Miss LeHand is a lady of rare ability and charms."

Locals, and many others, wondered about the relationship between LeHand and Roosevelt. Some thought that in addition to their boss-employee relationship, they were great friends, while others suspected a romantic relationship. Many thought that LeHand was in love with Roosevelt. Sadly, she had difficult times during her years working with Roosevelt. She apparently had a mental breakdown during a visit to Warm Springs in 1927. She was ill for much of that year but appears to have fully recovered by winter. Several authors have speculated that one possible cause of her depression was the reappearance of Lucy Mercer Rutherfurd in Roosevelt's life. Correspondence found in 2005 indicate that they at least stayed in touch through letters. LeHand had long since accepted Mrs. Roosevelt as an important, if often absent, part of his life. Knowing that Rutherfurd, his earlier love, was also part of the scene may have caused LeHand to become severely depressed.

Tragically, Missy LeHand suffered two strokes in 1941 that left her paralyzed at the age of forty-three. After that time, Roosevelt spent few days in Georgia. The pressures of guiding the United States through the Second World War plus LeHand's condition may have lessened the president's desire to visit Warm Springs. Missy LeHand died on July 31, 1944.[25]

THIS PHOTOGRAPH, taken during a peaceful moment at Warm Springs in 1931, shows New York governor Franklin D. Roosevelt reading the *New York Times*. In an interview seven years earlier, during his first visit to Warm Springs, Roosevelt delighted in the fact that it took two to three days to receive news from the rest of the world. As his responsibilities grew, the arrival of mail and newspapers necessarily became more prompt.

MANY PEOPLE IN GEORGIA and the nation saw Roosevelt standing on the back of a train, as he did in a photograph with his son James, or through the windows of railroad cars. Others gathered at railroad stations to see him getting on or off the train, as one photograph caught him doing while talking to Fred Botts. During train travel, Roosevelt would often smile and wave at those gathered along the tracks. At other times, an assistant would wear a similar hat, sit in his seat, and wave.

Myrtice Chauncey remembered when Roosevelt came through tiny Offerman in Pierce County. She was about twelve and saw Roosevelt after he had spoken at Memorial Stadium in Savannah. The town had a railroad crossing where north-south tracks going from Savannah to Jacksonville joined with the east-west tracks, which carried the president back to Warm Springs. Word had spread that Roosevelt would be traveling through town, and about fifty people gathered to see him. His train came up the curved tracks, stopped, and was switched to the Atlantic, Birmingham and Coast tracks heading west.

When the train pulled up, Roosevelt had his back to the crowd. An aide adjusted his chair, and he nodded and smiled at those gathered. He was not wearing his jacket or his hat. An aide motioned to Melvin Davis. Over the noise of the train, Davis pointed out the former location of an old sawmill, which had once been one of the largest in the Southeast. The aide then went back into the train and shared this information with the president.

At the beginning of the twentieth century, harvesting timber had been one of the largest industries in South Georgia. Roosevelt may have stopped in Offerman that day simply because there were no direct routes between Savannah and

Warm Springs. Another possibility is that he had gotten to know Chauncey's uncle, Lewis Cartier, an Offerman native who had moved to Manchester, owned a hardware store, and worked at the Little White House. His stories about the huge lumberyard might have explained the president's curiosity.[26]

Roosevelt used his time on trains to work and meet with fellow politicians and business leaders. Legislators and supporters would often board his train shortly before events. C. R. Adamson, a conductor based in Atlanta in the 1930s, remembered meeting the president: "I've hauled President Roosevelt. He asked me to come in the drawing room and talk with him. He wanted to find out how I liked my job and what my work was and everything."[27] Roosevelt met with Atlanta mayor William Hartsfield several times during his stops at Terminal Station in Atlanta. In a biography of Hartsfield, Harold Martin states that the mayor remembered that the president "would start talking as soon as Hartsfield entered the 'Ferdinand Magellan,' the President's private car, and would talk without ceasing until the train bumped and Marvin McIntyre told Hartsfield it was time to leave. Roosevelt was perhaps the only man with whom the talkative Hartsfield was never able to get in a word edgewise."[28]

FORMER NEW YORK STATE TROOPER Earl R. Miller (shown with the president poolside) served Roosevelt as trainer, confidant, and bodyguard. With such help, Roosevelt became an expert swimmer and developed significant upper-body strength. Roosevelt enjoyed swimming and sitting in the sun. Paul Rogers, a polio patient who first visited Warm Springs in 1925 or 1926, recalled: "I came down and of course in the early days we had no regular treatment although they did get us physical therapists and so we had treatment down at the old public pool . . . in general, building up . . . health and being able to use what [muscles] I have left."[29]

Miller; fellow bodyguard Gus Gennerich, a former New York City policeman; and Roosevelt's sons became quite skilled at helping "the boss" in and out of cars and assisting him in public so that Roosevelt appeared to be walking mostly on his own. (Miller later served as a bodyguard for Eleanor Roosevelt, and their close friendship became the subject of much gossip.)

GOVERNOR FRANKLIN D. ROOSEVELT relaxes for a moment in 1929 in the middle of his first term as governor at his Warm Springs home, later known as McCarthy Cottage. He had unofficially begun to run for president of the United States, and the focus of his speeches had shifted to national issues. In addressing the Atlanta Bar Association on May 9, 1929, he talked about criminal justice and punishment. He stated: "There has been a growing conviction in all parts of the country that the Administration of Justice is not keeping pace with the changing conditions of civilization. . . . More and more members of the Bench and Bar are subscribing to the somewhat new opinion that there is nothing sacred about the law which requires that it shall not be changed. . . . Some states have tried of late years to strengthen the law by recognizing the gravity of second and third and fourth offenses against the criminal law."[30]

New York had recently enacted such laws, which Roosevelt believed acted as deterrents against "professional and habitual criminals." He also urged states to move toward a "greater uniformity of laws." He concluded by stressing the importance of adapting to societal changes, codifying laws, and handing out consistent justice by saying: "The questions involved do not affect mere lawyers, they affect the body politic, the men, women, and children in every walk of life, in farm and in city." He concluded with words that contrasted with his actions in the next decade by stating that the federal government could not handle all the "difficult and complex state problems. . . . It [was] time to reassert the initiative of local and state governments."[31]

Roosevelt also mentioned societal changes during this speech. "Life today means new occupations, new thoughts, new contacts. . . . The best example is the wholly changed position of women in their relationship to the family and the community." He may have been talking about his wife, who was a teacher, a co-owner of the Todhunter School in New York, and a frequent speaker at civic and political gatherings. She certainly did not fit the image of the traditional wife and mother at this point in their marriage.

ROOSEVELT often attracted children. As he drove his car in November 1930, he stopped to visit with two boys, Hugh Love (left) and Walter Carpenter. On another occasion the governor was photographed with Arthur Carpenter Jr. and his dog, Wolf. Carpenter's father served as business manager at the foundation.

In *The Secret Diary of Harold L. Ickes*, the secretary of the interior recalled a trip to Warm Springs in November 1933. "The President is always charming but he was delightful at Warm Springs. Everyone there loves him, and crowds hang outside the gate, especially on Sundays, just to see him and cheer him as he drives in and out occasionally. . . . I have never had contact with a man who was loved as he is. To the people of Warm Springs he is just a big jolly brother."[32]

William Hanson, an area resident, remembered talking to Roosevelt when he was about twelve. "He always liked children. He asked what we were going to be when we grew up. . . . Well whatever you are going to be, be prepared to give more to your country than has ever been given before." (Ironically, a few years later, Hanson was one of the Fort Benning soldiers who marched with Roosevelt's funeral procession before the train carrying his body left Warm Springs for the final time in April 1945.)[33]

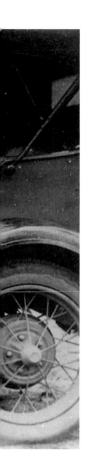

ON WEDNESDAY, DECEMBER 3, 1930, Governor Roosevelt addressed two hundred members of the Overseers' Club of Callaway Mills. Executives from plants in LaGrange, Hogansville, Manchester, and Milstead gathered at the Meriwether Inn. Shown in this photograph of Callaway Mills executives are, from left, Lee Talman; William Turner; Hatton Lovejoy, attorney for Callaway Mills; Roosevelt; Fuller E. Callaway Jr.; Edward Flynn, New York secretary of state; and H. W. Caldwell, a Troup County representative in the Georgia legislature.

Roosevelt told the group he wanted to talk about government, not politics. He began by humorously addressing Prohibition. He declared: "Despite the tottering steps of the eighteenth amendment, I do not believe Griffin will ever come back." He explained that a saloon and gambling house had once flourished in Warm Springs. A prominent resident would tell his wife he was going to Griffin, implying a town in nearby Spalding County. He would instead spend his day at a saloon. (The Twenty-First Amendment repealed the Eighteenth Amendment in December 1933.)

In introducing him, Lovejoy "praised the record of the New York governor and asserted that many Georgians hope[d] to see him inducted soon into the highest office of the country." Roosevelt urged governments to become more efficient like private businesses. He pointed out that while many complained about mounting costs, many more demands were now placed on government than had been made even thirty years earlier. He also mentioned that the public benefits from better treatment of prisoners, "mental defectives," and "cripples." "In the old days a cripple was said to be the result of an act of God. Think of the terrible things we used to lay on God, and never lifted a finger to remedy! Now better medical treatment is increasing the number of cripples who are being returned to useful life. All these things cost money." He challenged those present to pay more attention to their governments. "The first and last cause of government waste lies in the apathy of the electorate itself." He closed by denouncing demagogues. "The length of time you can fool all the people is getting shorter. Our greatest hope is that people like you will demand business efficiency in government that will keep us out of bankruptcy."[34]

Roosevelt had arrived at the station in Warm Springs on November 21, after having been elected to a second term as governor of New York. Supporters of the recently organized Warm Springs–Meriwether County Roosevelt for President Club, which already counted over fifteen hundred members, greeted him. In addressing the crowd at the depot, Governor Roosevelt stated: "I am not down here to rest from a strenuous campaign but to enjoy a delightful vacation among my Georgia friends and neighbors. I thank you for your welcome and I cherish the sentiments of friendship which you have expressed and which your presence here indicates."[35]

THE MERIWETHER COUNTY Roosevelt for President club hosted a "Roosevelt Homecoming Barbecue" on October 13, 1931. The Atlanta firemen sent a fifty-piece band to entertain the 1,500 to 2,000 people who paid seventy-five cents each to attend. The firemen had supported Roosevelt since 1929, when he had been one of the first to donate to their fund to purchase instruments. The event bore all the markings of a political affair, though the honoree told Dr. R. B. Gilbert, "I want to meet the people of Meriwether County; I want to shake their hands and know them. I do not want any politics mentioned at the 'cue.'" He added, "I want Sheriff Jake on the platform with two guns, and the first one who mentions politics—bang!"[36] The *Atlanta Journal* noted the attitude of one black man who dug a barbecue pit before the festivities: "Laway man, everybody around here's thinking 'bout Mr. Roosevelt being next president and taint likely they all going to keep still."[37]

Virtually all sixty or so Roosevelt for President clubs in Georgia sent representatives. The *Columbus Enquirer* reported: "Muscogee County will do its best today in 'welcoming home' the public man and adopted son whom many predict is going to be the next president of the United States."[38] The clubs also held an exhibition golf tournament.

At the barbecue, Roosevelt briefly addressed the crowd. "I have come to love this land of yours as a home—a place where I can come and rest and feel natural. You people in Georgia have something that I am not at all sure you realize—a great country, a fine land, and a place that every American should feel proud of." A member of the fireman's band then shouted, "Three cheers for President Roosevelt," at which the New Yorker reportedly "smiled tolerantly." In this photo are Georgia congressman W. C. Wright (standing behind Roosevelt on his left); Senator William J. Harris (on Roosevelt's immediate left), who also served in President Woodrow Wilson's administration; and J. T. Anderson of Milledgeville. Mrs. W. A. Williams of Warm Springs is refilling the governor's glass. Maj. John S. Cohen, a political leader and newsman, and Congressmen Eugene Cox and Carl Vinson also attended. Harris died six months later, and Cohen was appointed to serve as interim senator before elections could be held that fall.

The Atlanta firemen's band played a march composed by bandmaster Thomas Altobellies titled "Forward Franklin D. Roosevelt." The chorus went: "Let's win the fight with Roosevelt and lift his banner in the sky. We know he's meant for president so join the throng as we pass by."

AFTER BEING INTRODUCED, Roosevelt complemented the "splendid administration of [his] old, young friend, Gov. Richard B. Russell, Jr." (Russell had recently been elected governor of Georgia. He was the state's youngest governor in the twentieth century.) He expressed pleasure and pride in the "progress being made in this state as regards roads, educational improvements, and civic betterments in general, declaring that the people of Georgia were on the right track to solve their problems." He regretted the fact that many young people were leaving farms since "no one on the farms [was] going to starve this winter," alluding to the hard economic times of the early years of the Great Depression and the fact that young people were looking for more opportunities. He closed by assuring his friends that he hoped to "come back to [his] Georgia home" every year in the future.[39]

Roosevelt arrived in Warm Springs on October 2, 1931, for a two-week vacation. Missy LeHand, stenographer Margaret Donnally, aides Earl Miller and Gus Gennerich, and three newspapermen—James Kieran of the *New York Times*, William Lawley of the *New York American*, and Walter T. Brown of the Associated Press—traveled with him. A few days before the barbecue, delegations from Birmingham, Alabama, and Jackson, Mississippi, met Roosevelt at Warm Springs. William C. Fitts, a Birmingham attorney who had become friends with Roosevelt during World War I when he served as an assistant attorney general, stated: "There has been no organized effort to win support in Alabama for Mr. Roosevelt. It's not necessary. The folks over there like him and do their part, get together, and organize their own clubs."[40]

IN THIS December 7, 1931, photograph, Roosevelt works at his desk with his campaign manager James Farley standing immediately behind him. Charles Richard Crane, a former ambassador to China, joined them. According to the *Atlanta Journal*, the men did not reveal the subject of their meeting. Crane was a wealthy businessman whose primary interests were Eastern Europe and the Middle East. The men may have been discussing Palestinian affairs. The party left Warm Springs the next day and motored to Newnan to catch the Crescent Limited to Atlanta.[41]

THROUGHOUT HIS VISIT to Warm Springs in the fall of 1931, Roosevelt remained tight-lipped with reporters. He insisted that the "affairs of New York State exclusively and not national politics" occupied his time. Roosevelt responded to questions about whether he and New York Democratic state chairman James Farley would be discussing a national organization to promote his candidacy for president by stating: "I know nothing about any national organization. I'm too busy being governor of New York."[42]

Roosevelt and Farley are shown in this December 8 photograph relaxing in the living room of McCarthy Cottage. Two accessories there relate to the sea: the clock made like a ship's wheel and the model sailing vessel in the upper left. Both reflect Roosevelt's love of the ocean and the navy.

When traveling from New York State to Warm Springs, Farley stopped in Washington, DC, to visit members of Congress. He predicted that Roosevelt would win the Democratic nomination on the first ballot. Eleanor Roosevelt stopped in Atlanta on her way to Warm Springs and spoke at the Lovett School and addressed the League of Women Voters about the need for greater public awareness and education about government. Roosevelt made several exceptions to his rule of focusing on New York issues by meeting with local delegations promoting his candidacy for national office. He also spoke at a meeting of over one hundred men seeking an east-west highway in Georgia running through Savannah, Statesboro, Macon, Warm Springs, and West Point that would eventually connect to Seattle. (Forty-seven years later, Interstate 16 opened, covering the eastern part of the route from Macon to Savannah, though a direct connection between Macon, Warm Springs, and West Point on the Alabama line has never been built.) On December 10, Roosevelt headed back to New York and told reporters: "My stay in Warm Springs did me a world of good and I am feeling great."[43]

After many months of speculation, Roosevelt officially entered the race for president of the United States on January 29, 1932, when he allowed his name to be listed in the North Dakota presidential primary. Farley managed his 1932 campaign for president with assistance from longtime Roosevelt associate Louis Howe.

Roosevelt soon named W. E. Page, publisher of the *Columbus Ledger* and *Enquirer-Sun*, as his personal representative in Georgia "to act on his behalf relative to furthering his Presidential nomination," according to the *Warm Springs Mirror*. The Piedmont Hotel in Atlanta housed the state headquarters for the Roosevelt for President campaign. Page had been part of a Columbus group that befriended Roosevelt during his early days in Georgia.[44]

ROOSEVELT WROTE in the February 1931 issue of *Holiday*: "For the past six years, whenever the pressures of public duties and private affairs permitted, I have fled to Georgia for escape from the rigorous North and I have found in her hospitable climate peace and contentment, a release from the worries of the everyday, and a refreshment of body and spirit." He went on to point out that wealthy families had been visiting Georgia for years, frequenting Jekyll Island, Cumberland Island, Sapelo Island, and elsewhere, noting: "But now when it is at last possible to go from one end of the State to the other without leaving concrete, those of more moderate means are finding out the many delights of Georgia." He described the Warm Springs region as having "good bird-shooting and the finest horseback riding imaginable. Golf is a latecomer here but good links are being laid out. There is nothing mythical about the hospitality of the people . . . once they are convinced of your genuine friendship, will almost literally give you the shirts off their backs." He ended by observing that Georgia was rapidly moving forward, proud of its past but ready to deal with its problems, including "shifting from cotton to diversified crops . . . improving conditions in cotton mills," and more.

Here Arthur Carpenter (right), business manager at Warm Springs, and Les Kibbe, an engineer, join Roosevelt as he turns on the water atop the hill above the foundation. Carpenter developed polio in 1927 and was dependent on an iron lung. Keith Morgan, a close friend of both Carpenter and Basil O'Connor, encouraged him to seek treatment at Warm Springs. Following treatment, Carpenter stayed on staff until 1935, when he became executive director of the national foundation. Like Roosevelt and other polio victims, he developed tremendous upper-body strength. Morgan also joined the staff at the Warm Springs Foundation, serving as director of public relations. As liberal Democrats from New York State, both Morgan and Carpenter strongly supported Roosevelt the political leader.[45]

ALICE PLASTRIDGE shared a story: "I think one of the funniest things that I ever saw was one time when [Roosevelt] was going across the campus there weaving in and out between the trees [in his car] so the secret service men couldn't follow him in the big car."[46]

Victimized by polio as a young boy, Judge Frank Cheatham received treatment at the Warm Springs Foundation and later remembered: "I'm told the President thought it was great sport to elude his bodyguards. The area around the Little White House had a lot of small winding dirt roads. On at least one occasion, he was able to lose them. They finally found him and scolded the President as much as you can scold the President of the United States."[47]

In this photograph, Roosevelt holds his cigarette in his customary long holder. Tom Rush worked as a push boy at the Warm Springs Foundation. "I asked him about that long cigarette holder. I asked him why he had such a long one and he said the doctor told him to stay as far away from cigarettes as possible."[48]

VISITS TO WARM SPRINGS provided Roosevelt time to develop goals, such as when New York officials joined him there following the 1928 election, or to plot strategy, such as in his meetings with campaign manager James Farley. Here, in the fall of 1931, Roosevelt discusses activities of the Warm Springs Foundation and possibly a campaign contribution with businessman Bernarr Macfadden. Many considered this visitor either a "health nut" or a "health guru" who championed physical exercise and diet reform as publisher of *Physical Culture*, a popular magazine. While at Warm Springs, Macfadden visited with Roosevelt, inspected his cattle herd, swam in the Warm Springs pools, and learned about patient treatment. Macfadden achieved significant financial success by publishing a variety of magazines and books. Over the years, he sought but never gained positions as secretary of health, governor of Florida, and president of the United States.

IN A RELAXED MOMENT, Roosevelt enjoys a sunny Georgia day with three local children, from right, Constance Bradley, Diana Patterson, and Hugh Love. Though the press corps accompanied Roosevelt to Warm Springs, they respected his privacy and handicap and took pictures only at specific times and places. In most photographs, Roosevelt wore a tie, usually with a coat, reflecting his professional position and upper-class upbringing. Here he sports a style more fitting a relaxing vacation.

Roosevelt was the father of six children born between 1906 and 1916, five of whom lived to adulthood. Both Franklin and Eleanor spent extended periods away from their own children in the 1920s, yet children loved Franklin. Claude Bray Jr., who later served as a state representative from Meriwether County, remembered that "children were just drawn to Roosevelt because he loved them and children can sense when you like them. . . . He was their buddy. . . . He was an inspiration to them. He taught them that here at Warm Springs . . . disabilities can be prevented from becoming handicaps."[49]

ELABORATE BUT INFORMAL picnics became very popular in Warm Springs during Roosevelt's visits. Men and women dressed up to eat outside, often on a hillside. In one photo taken at Dowdell's Knob on Pine Mountain, a favorite picnic spot, Roosevelt shares a bench with polio patient Elizabeth Whitehead Pearson. In another, Missy LeHand can be seen on the far right, wearing sunglasses.

Roosevelt loved the land around Warm Springs. In an April 18, 1925, Roosevelt Says newspaper column, he reported on a visit to Dowdell's Knob. "Yesterday afternoon I went to the top of Pine Mountain. There, stretching out for many miles to the horizon, was a large portion of Meriwether County. It was good looking country—and good to live in. In many ways, it reminded me of the views I get from hill tops in my own Dutchess County, back from the Hudson River."

Dr. and Mrs. Hal Raper remembered a picnic at Dowdell's Knob in the late 1930s or early 1940s. "There were no chairs. We took the seats in the cars out. . . . We each had some conversation with the President. We talked about anything and everything." Olive Carpenter Johnson (widow of Arthur Carpenter, manager of the foundation) added: "The picnics were ordinary picnics like you and I would have. Hot dogs and rolls and pickles, maybe a salad and coffee. . . . Missy, his secretary, used to call up and say 'we are going for a ride this evening, the boss and I are going for a ride. Will you and Carp come along with us?' We used to go quite frequently." She added that one of the main reasons Roosevelt liked to go on these rides was that "he loved people, people as they were. . . . Roosevelt was so kind and cordial. . . . He never said a word . . . if their language wasn't quite correct."[50]

Among those attending the picnic shown in the lower two photos are Eleanor, S. Chevalier, Marvin McIntyre and Dr. Ross McIntire, the president's secretary and doctor, a Mrs. Scherber, and Dorothy Brown. Chevalier was a nationally known corporate tax attorney who suffered from polio.

IN MAY 1930, daughter Anna Dall, son James, and his wife, Betsy Cushing (on left), joined Roosevelt in this casual family portrait at Warm Springs. Decades later, Anna remembered the vigor that her father always exuded. Both people who knew him and those who had never met the president noted his strong personality and his energy. People saw him sitting down or leaning against a podium and seldom thought of his physical problems.[51]

James Mackay, a member of the Georgia and the U.S. House of Representatives during the 1950s and 1960s, remembered Roosevelt and the freedom he had when driving his car:

> They said that the wonderful thing about this man is that he was never the big shot in the house. He wanted to know who was in the kitchen, and what the chauffeur was being expected to do, and that was reflected in his activities at Warm Springs when he would sneak off from the Secret Service. I heard James Roosevelt say this on the twenty-fifth anniversary of his death, that his daddy was the last President of the United States that had the privilege of independently riding down the road and just driving up and asking somebody what they thought about things, and that security had destroyed all that. He was saying that he thought that it was important to govern, to be able to be in touch with the people.[52]

FISHING THE RIVERS AND CREEKS

of Georgia may have been a pastime that Roosevelt enjoyed for the same reasons fishermen continue to enjoy the sport: having an opportunity to be outdoors, escaping from day-to-day worries, and being able to catch fish. Alternately, photos of Roosevelt dating from the late 1920s and early 1930s may have just been part of a concerted effort to show the New York governor as physically active.

In this 1930 photo, Roosevelt sits on a car seat as he fishes the Flint River in the Meriwether County area known as "the Cove." He talks with an unidentified woman while the puppy seems more interested in the can of bait than his distinguished company. Roosevelt had visited the area in December 1928 and was entertained by Bun Wright, who played "old-time music" on his fiddle. In November 1934, President Roosevelt and his party had a fish fry at Flat Shoals on the Flint River. Arthur Carpenter wrote Roosevelt's secretary Marvin McIntyre: "The plan is to leave the pool at 12:30 and drive directly to Flat Shoals. I appreciate your offer to get word to members of your staff, the press, photographers, etc." The picnic ended up with at least twenty-eight additional guests; simple outings with the president rarely happened. Roosevelt mentioned several times that the area would make an especially attractive recreational site.

ROOSEVELT ENJOYS A SANDWICH as he takes a break from fishing the Flint River in May 1930. Fellow picnickers sit on car seats as two men hold the long board that serves as a table. Coats and ties seem to be the expected dress for this fishing expedition.

ROOSEVELT GREW UP riding and owning horses in New York State. After he was stricken with polio, he rode at least a few times. In his book *The Story of Warm Springs*, Turnley Walker reports that Roosevelt and Fred Botts, a fellow polio patient, found the site for Roosevelt's new home, which became known as the Little White House, while riding horses.

Roosevelt may have been forty years ahead of his time by being one of the first therapeutic horseback riders in the United States. Horseback riding would have helped the circulation in his legs. Riding would also have helped with improving motor skills, balance, and coordination. Roosevelt and other polio victims, especially those in wheelchairs, may also have liked sitting so high in the air astride a horse. Here, Roosevelt rides with Earl Miller, while aide Gus Gennerich stands nearby in case of problems.

Uncertainty remains about whether Roosevelt actually enjoyed horseback riding or rode just so that photographs proving his physical fitness could be snapped. He looked uncomfortable on the back of the horse. In *This I Remember*, Eleanor Roosevelt recalls that Earl Miller, a New York State trooper, decided it would be good for Franklin to ride horseback again. He also thought Missy LeHand and Eleanor should ride. After having ridden sidesaddle in her youth, Eleanor eventually began to feel comfortable riding horses as an adult and continued to ride for many years. She adds: "My husband was not able to get any pleasure out of riding after he became paralyzed, though he had been a fine horseman . . . he never got over his sense of insecurity in the saddle, because he could not use the muscles necessary to balance himself on a horse."[53]

In *Franklin D. Roosevelt: A Career in Progressive Democracy*, Ernest Lindley writes, "Since he became Governor, he has taken up horseback riding again, and has begun to develop a grip with his knees—although he still keeps the horse at a walk."[54] Lindley often joined two or three other journalists to travel with Roosevelt to Warm Springs. The saddle had no modifications to make it easier for Roosevelt to ride. Roosevelt kept horses at Warm Springs and maintained stables. Area youth, such as Arthur Carpenter's sons and Bill Trotter, son of the manager of Callaway Mills in Manchester, were allowed to ride his horses when they wanted.

In a newspaper interview on October 18, 1930, Roosevelt mentions obtaining a $500,000 life insurance policy with the Georgia Warm Springs Foundation named as beneficiary. Dr. E. W. Beckwith, medical director of the Equitable Life Assurance Society, which issued the policy, praised the governor's physical condition. In answering a reporter's questions about how he maintained his health, Roosevelt credited his daily swims and horseback rides, both of which he pursued in New York and Warm Springs.[55]

WHEN SPEAKING TO GROUPS, Roosevelt often referred to himself as a farmer from Dutchess County, New York. Farmers faced tough economic times in the 1920s and 1930s, thanks in part to the boll weevil, the Depression, and the dust bowl. Roosevelt wanted to show farmers how to improve their land and save their agrarian way of life. Part of his property in Georgia contained peach trees, but after a trial period, he rejected the fruit as one of his main crops and concentrated instead on grapes, tomatoes, and sweet potatoes. His gardens produced some of the fruits and vegetables consumed at the Warm Springs Foundation, while other crops from the farm were sold in the Atlanta area. Clark Howell reported: "One of his orders is: 'Don't shop around. Sell on the local market.'"[56] Local residents felt that the farm experienced more problems after Roosevelt became president and had to rely more heavily on farm managers, though the worsening national economy also made profitable farming more difficult.

Otis Moore, Roosevelt's farm manager, reflected in the 1960s: "People in this country didn't know you could set out a pine. We did it. But the first ones we put out were longleaf. We learned that this was not the best tree, because it took too long to grow; also there is not much sale for longleaf around here. . . . We found out later that loblolly is the best; it grows faster and you can work it better."[57]

In this carefully posed photo, Roosevelt uses a handsaw to remove the lower limbs from a hardwood tree. Roosevelt loved trees but considered them just another crop to use on the farm. He felt they should be harvested for lumber and even as wood for fires. He told local farmer Jess Long to sell some of his trees when the Civilian Conservation Corp camp was building the road between Warm Springs and Pine Mountain. Long remembered Roosevelt saying, "Now, Jess, there is lots of wood on this mountain. You might as well sell wood to the CCC camp," adding, "And that is what I did during the entire time they were here."[58]

In an interview in 1950, Arthur Carpenter reported that Roosevelt was "a nut on trees." He had a portion of his Warm Springs property planted with longleaf pine trees and checked on their growth each visit. He urged neighbors to plant trees that would "save their soil, bring them more money and better lives."[59] He thought that a tree should never be cut on his own property or on the foundation's lands if it could be spared, though his farm manager harvested timber from his property each year.

Roosevelt went further than planting trees when he and Georgia governor L. G. Hardmann organized the first fire prevention unit in Meriwether County in 1929. The program included a demonstration tree planting of longleaf pine seedlings and talks about the destructive force of forest fires. The following year, he dedicated a fire tower on top of Pine Mountain. The Meriwether County fire prevention organization took over tower operations after the ceremonies. Roosevelt made a brief speech stating that he hoped the tower helped Meriwether County become "the forerunner of a movement which [would] spread over the state for the conservation of our forests." He went on to say that "the Georgia Warm Springs Foundation was also a conservation organization, specializing in the conservation of health among the young people."[60] On November 29, 1932, just three weeks after being elected president of the United States, Roosevelt addressed a meeting of the Meriwether Forest and Fire Prevention Organization that also featured a report by Dr. Charles H. Herty on his experiments using southern pine to produce quality newsprint and bond papers. Roosevelt urged federal and state cooperation in forestry conservation in every state in the union.[61]

In February 1934, Roosevelt purchased 473 acres of land adjoining foundation property from Georgia Wilkins. With the purchase, he told Herman Swift, a Columbus attorney who negotiated the deal: "Tell Miss Georgia that my one hope is that we can keep the fires out of this property. There is an increasing seeding of longleaf pines. I hope too that we can build some more roads to act as fire breaks. My only regret is that I cannot be there more to superintend the work."[62]

ON NOVEMBER 29, 1930, two days after Thanksgiving dinner at Warm Springs, Roosevelt participated in a possum hunt and dinner widely celebrated by the press. The Atlanta Association of Property Owners and Managers originally scheduled the event to be at the home of Benson Tigner. His granddaughter Martha recalls that they moved the dinner because "it got so big with Democrats all over wanting to come that they decided to have it at the White Sulphur Springs Hotel." One hundred sixty-nine guests attended. Tigner's son, J. Hope, had once owned the hotel located west of Warm Springs and was a member of the association. Before the dinner, Tigner took his family to Warm Springs to finalize plans and meet Roosevelt. In this photograph, sisters Martha and Adalaide Tigner visit with the governor. As Adalaide looks on, Roosevelt and seventeen-year-old old Martha pull the tails of two possums. Martha reported, "[This was] the only possum I ever had contact with. . . . I never held a possum. . . . I'd never seen one before but I said I'd hold one." A man put the possums in the tree and instructed Miss Tigner and Roosevelt to hold the critters.[63]

J. HOPE TIGNER AND ROOSEVELT enjoyed the possum and taters dinner. This photograph shows Martha Tigner serving them as a waiter moves in the background. Newspapers reported that this was the first possum Roosevelt had ever consumed though he had reported in 1925 that he had a possum dinner on his first trip to Georgia in 1913 when he visited Brunswick. Though possum was served, the menu also featured "Meriwether Baked Plymouth Hen," biscuits, sweet potato pudding, and pecan pie. Martha Tigner reported: "Many of Atlanta's most prominent folks were there. . . . They put on a really good show. . . . Everybody got up and made speeches. . . . Roosevelt talked about differences between hospitality in Georgia and other places in the East. . . . Everybody had a good time."[64]

Others in attendance included Georgia governor-elect Richard B. Russell Jr., Judge J. R. Terrell of Greenville, and non-Georgians Missy LeHand, New Yorker Edward Flynn and his wife, and reporters from the *New York American* and the *New York World*. Eleanor Roosevelt and her friend Nancy Cook attended, though she was barely mentioned in the publicity. According to Martha Tigner, the hosts, the Atlanta Association of Owners and Builders, assumed that no one else would honor Governor Roosevelt with a possum dinner. They actually followed a short-lived Georgia presidential tradition. On January 15, 1909, Atlantans treated President William Howard Taft to a possum dinner at the Atlanta Municipal Auditorium and Armory.

When asked about her memories of Roosevelt, Tigner stated: "I loved him. . . . I remember when he shook my hand and looked at me and said, 'Hello Martha.' I was sunk, melted away. . . . He really had the most wonderful personality. . . . We didn't notice [his disability]. We all knew he had polio, but that was not the main thing. It was his personality that shone through."[65]

ROOSEVELT PARTICIPATED in the possum hunt from the comfort of his car. Coon dogs appear to have treed a possum as neighbors were coming for the hunt that took place after dinner. After the crowd gathered, Roosevelt drove up to the hunting scene. For the occasion, Roosevelt smoked a corncob pipe rather than his usual cigarette and joined others in leaving his suit and tie at home.

At dinner, Roosevelt talked about the hospitality he had found at Warm Springs. On his first visit, locals welcomed him with a kitchen full of food. Ruth Stevens, in her book *"Hi-Ya, Neighbor,"* states: "He spoke of going to a town in New England where no one came to meet him nor to see him, nor did they give a cordial 'Howdy.' He paid a glowing tribute to our people and said he was always glad to come to his Georgia home. He said that he hoped to spend more time at his Warm Springs home . . . and that he would employ all his efforts in the interest of progress in this section."[66]

Martha Tigner remembered the possum hunt: "They were showing that Roosevelt was an active person. That was the thing to show that he could even go to a possum hunt . . . and showing that he could get around and do whatever he wanted even though he was paralyzed. . . . He charmed everyone, absolutely."[67]

Clark Howell, editor of the *Atlanta Constitution*, sent an introduction declaring that he felt certain the group was entertaining the next president of the United States. Charles F. Palmer, an Atlanta developer and president of the association, acted as toastmaster. A few years later, Palmer spearheaded the development of Techwood and University Homes, Atlanta slum-clearance projects.

THE POSSUM DINNER and hunt proved to be a big hit in the media; nonetheless, Roosevelt had to defend his possum hunt. After receiving widespread publicity about the hunt, he told journalists: "I believe I received 500 letters from people protesting against the cruelty of great big men and fierce looking dogs murdering a poor, defenseless, pathetic looking little animal like a 'possum. . . . Finally in self-defense, I had to write . . . a letter explaining that we didn't hurt the 'possum at all, but picked out a big tree where he was safe from the dogs, turned him loose and wished him well in this era of food shortage." He declared that this southern tradition was not understood in the Northeast, but when asked if he would go on another hunt, the governor responded, "Well, just invite me."[68]

Several years later, Roosevelt decided to have more fun with possums. Lizzy McDuffie, Roosevelt's housekeeper, remembered a very cold day in Warm Springs when he decided to play a trick on the press. He sent word that they should gather at the Little White House early one cold morning. They rushed over with coats, cameras, and notepads and were led out behind the house. Roosevelt then declared the gathering to be the dedication of the "Secretary Marvin McIntyre Possum Preserve." He joked that the preserve would help prevent the extinction of a great American symbol of freedom, the possum. The president thoroughly enjoyed himself, but the members of the press were not thrilled. McDuffie worked for the president for eighteen years, and her husband, Irvin, served as his valet and barber for twelve years. They also served as conduits for information and access between Walter White and the NAACP and White House officials.[69]

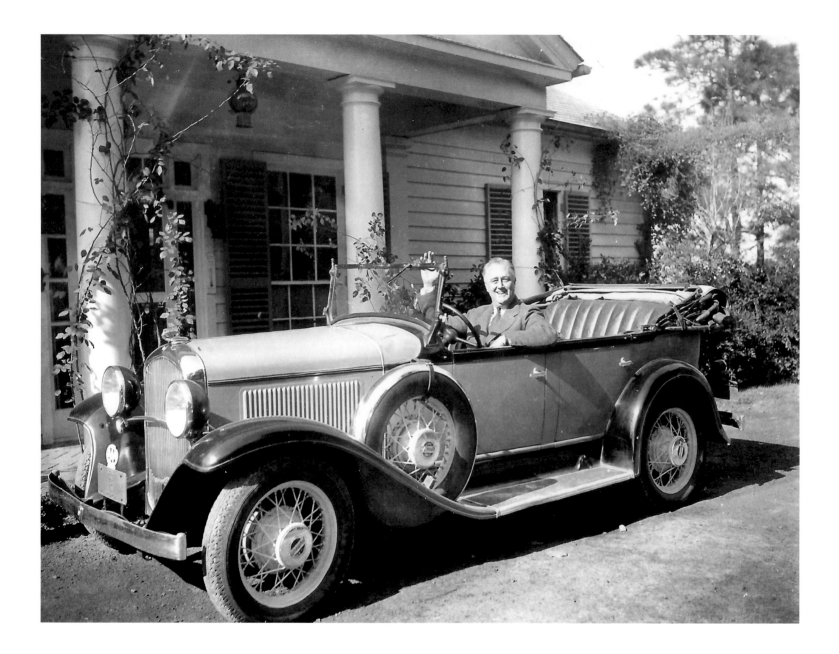

ROOSEVELT WAVES from behind the steering wheel of his 1932 Model A Plymouth in front of the Little White House. Local residents became so accustomed to seeing him driving area roads that they quipped that he was as regular as the mailman. His neighborly approach had benefits beyond staying in touch with friends and local citizens. Roosevelt could pull up in front of the Warm Springs drugstore for sodas served via "Presidential Curb Service."[70]

Downing Musgrove, executive secretary for Governor E. D. Rivers, remembered driving from Atlanta to Warm Springs with some of Roosevelt's guests, such as Harry Hopkins and John H. Bankhead. "We'd get down to the Little White House properties, and there was a round circular driveway with some shaded area there . . . and in a few minutes you'd hear this little car coming up and you'd look and the President was coming in that little—I think it was a Plymouth. . . . It had a little honk, honk horn on the side of it. . . . He'd come pull into that circle. He was just waving and speaking to everybody. . . . He would joke with you. He'd make funny remarks and kid with the people who were arriving."[71]

Martha Tigner reported that "Grandpa [Benson Tigner of nearby White Sulphur Springs] was in his nineties. He was in a wheelchair. Roosevelt would come up to the farm house and blow his horn, and they would wheel Grandpa out to the gate and they would talk." Suzanne Pike, a young girl who grew up in Meriwether County, recalled: "When the President drove up . . . he just stopped right in front of the house. . . . I thought this was the biggest thrill because he stopped. . . . He wanted to find out about the farm."[72]

Roosevelt enjoyed his cars. In 1940, a new car arrived for the president: a Willys roadster with new and radically different hand controls. He sent word to Fred Botts: "Please tell Fred that I understood the hand control on this new car was to be just like the controls I use now. . . . This car is to remain at Warm Springs for my use when I am there but to be used by Fred when I am not there. Incidentally, tell Fred that the license and accident insurance on the car should be taken out by the Foundation as it will be used by the Foundation 95% of the year."[73]

ON MARCH 23, Roosevelt won the primary in Georgia. He told the press: "I am particularly happy by the Georgia vote and I deeply appreciate the confidence shown in me by what I am proud to call 'my other state.'"[74] Citizens of Meriwether County cast 718 votes for Roosevelt versus 2 cast for his opponent.

He arrived in Georgia on April 30, ready to start his vacation and publicly announcing that he intended to rest throughout the trip. "I feel better already and I am glad to get back to the state that went for me ten to one."[75] In

reality, Roosevelt started spending more hours at Warm Springs working and less time exercising or resting. On one occasion he worked outdoors on the porch of his new home—which soon became known as the Little White House—with Eleanor at his side, along with their daughter-in-law Elizabeth "Betty" Donner, a wealthy Philadelphia socialite whose father owned Donner Steel Company. Son Elliott and Betty had married earlier that year.

Roosevelt stayed at Warm Springs for twenty-five days, taking a long break from his campaign for the Democratic nomination for president. John Nance Garner had just won the California contest, making a Roosevelt victory on the first ballot less likely. He officially remained silent on the political situation, though he met with numerous advisors and supporters.

Often, large crowds would quickly gather around Roosevelt. In May, Roosevelt told the National Patients Committee in Warm Springs: "I would rather be at Warm Springs than at Albany or anywhere else. The Foundation is something permanent and its usefulness will last forever, not merely for two or four years." Lewis Thornton of Wellsville, New York, president of the patients group, stated: "History will recognize with honor his versatile services to his country. But to us, patients at Warm Springs, no brilliant statescraft of his, no wise and popular policy, no inspired leadership, however wide reaching their benefits can equal in importance the noble example of his pure generosity and humanitarian interests."[76] At Warm Springs, Roosevelt had both time to relax and time to speak to large crowds.

THE NEW HOME occupied a higher, more secluded spot away from the institute grounds. Marines stood guard at sentry cottages around the home whenever the president was in residence. Roosevelt kept the furnishings at his Warm Springs residences simple. Virginia Shipp recalled: "My husband was Executive housekeeper here. He had charge of all the furnishings. . . . He noticed the silverware was in very poor condition. He asked Roosevelt if he wanted to pick out a new pattern and replace it. Roosevelt replied 'you know I eat with this silverware every day when I'm in Warm Springs. If anyone doesn't like it, he doesn't have to eat with me. I am satisfied.'"[77]

Roosevelt and architect Henry Toombs developed plans for this home. Other homes he lived in, including Springwood in Hyde Park, houses in Campobello and New York City, and the White House, had been built for others. Daniel Lumber Company of LaGrange constructed the Little White House and nearby garage for $7,350. Walter Doyle remembered bicycling out to the site every afternoon to check on progress. He considered himself the "sidewalk superintendent." The *Warm Springs Mirror* reported that the home had a direct phone line to New York, enabling the governor to stay in constant touch with his home state.

In an economical fashion, Roosevelt's cottage remained occupied in his absence. Surgeon-in-chief Dr. Michael Hoke lived there from 1932 until he resigned in September 1936. He vacated the premises whenever the president visited. Staff members often stayed at his old house, McCarthy Cottage, during visits.

A housewarming was held on Thursday, May 5. Between five hundred and a thousand guests attended as Mrs. Roosevelt and daughter-in-law Betty welcomed neighbors in the living room and the governor shook hands on the back porch. Visitors included area residents as well as polio patients. Foundation staff served lemonade and cookies.

The *Meriwether Vindicator* declared: "Their new home is pretty and convenient. The rear of it hangs over a precipice and from the porch commands a view of hill and dale for many miles." Mrs. Blon Williams, of Woodbury, presented Roosevelt with a large cake inscribed "Our Next President," while W. S. Simms and former sheriff Jake Jarrell gave him a cane inscribed "More Support from Meriwether County." National politics entered discussions when the guests at the housewarming learned that Senator Huey P. Long and the Louisiana delegation had announced they would stand behind Roosevelt at the Democratic Convention. Roosevelt refused comment, maintaining his stance of enjoying a nonpolitical vacation.[78]

Frances Perkins, Roosevelt's labor secretary, reflected several years later: "This capacity to entertain the great and the simple, the important and the unimportant of the earth with the same comfortable hospitality made a contribution. . . . Ninety-five percent of Americans felt they too could have visited in his home and been as comfortable."[79]

In January 1933, Arthur Carpenter sent Missy LeHand a statement of the governor's personal account for 1932. Roosevelt paid for his own home and expenses, though bills passed through the Warm Springs Foundation. Carp added a note cautioning, "If you are shocked by the size of the grocery item during the week of May 6th to 12th, let me explain that it included about $30.00 expense for the House Warming."[80]

Much of the furniture in the Little White House came from Val-Kill Industries, which Eleanor and three women partners had started in Hyde Park. They made reproductions of colonial-style furniture and metalwork and wanted to use the crafts as a way of increasing employment. Eleanor had chairs, chests of drawers, tables, and other pieces from Val-Kill shipped to Warm Springs to help furnish the new house. (Many of these pieces remain there today.)[81]

WHILE THE PRESS kept the public informed about Roosevelt's activities at Warm Springs, details often remain sketchy. A brief notice in the May 7 *Atlanta Journal* stated that "Saturday, the Governor was to have as his guest Joseph Kennedy of Boston, son-in-law of John Fitzgerald, former mayor of Boston and a Smith delegate to the Chicago Convention." Roosevelt solicited financial support for his presidential campaign. According to later accounts by Kennedy, he agreed to contribute $50,000 to Roosevelt's campaign and later raised another $150,000. Other reports indicate that Kennedy's total contribution to the first two presidential campaigns amounted to $360,000. (In 2014 dollars, this amount equals approximately $5.7 million.) Kennedy helped secure William Randolph Hearst's support during the 1932 Democratic Convention, thus assuring Roosevelt the nomination.

Roosevelt and Kennedy first met in 1930 when Hyde Park neighbor and advisor Henry Morgenthau Jr. brought the Boston businessman and Hollywood mogul to the governor's Mansion in Albany. Following Roosevelt's election as president, Kennedy, the son of Irish immigrants, served as head of the new Securities and Exchange Commission, head of the Maritime Commission, and U.S. ambassador to the Court of St. James. Throughout their years of contact, the president sought Kennedy's financial and verbal support, while Kennedy wanted the power that came with government positions. Kennedy (in the back row center) joined Roosevelt, Missy LeHand (on left), and newsmen Walter Brown, Jim Kieran, Ernest K. Lindley, and Lou Ruppel at a hillside picnic. Roosevelt wears a hat given him that weekend by visiting oilmen from Texas. (The ambassador's son John became the thirty-fifth president of the United States in 1961. John spoke at the Little White House just two and a half weeks before that presidential election.)

ON MAY 22, 1932, Oglethorpe University awarded Democratic presidential candidate Franklin D. Roosevelt an honorary doctoral degree. Roosevelt responded by giving a forceful commencement address that some consider to be his most effective speech ever.[82] Speaking at the Fox Theater, he called for "bold persistent experimentation." He wanted a "larger measure of social planning," stating, "We cannot allow our economic life to be controlled by that small group of men whose chief outlook upon social welfare is tinctured by the fact that they can make huge profits from the lending of money and the marketing of securities," referring to Wall Street financiers. He further emphasized the need to "inject life into our ailing economic order" by proposing a "wider, more equitable distribution of the national income." He declared: "I do not mean to intimate that we have come to the end of this period of expansion. We shall continue to need capital for expansion. We shall continue to need capital for the production of newly-invented devices, for the replacement of equipment worn out or rendered obsolete by our technical progress; we need better housing in many of our cities and we still need in many parts of the country more good roads, canals, parks and other improvements. . . . The country needs, and unless I mistake its temper, the country demands bold, persistent experimentation. It is common sense to make a method and try it: If it fails, admit it frankly and try another. But above all, try something."[83]

Roosevelt spoke at Oglethorpe after being invited by Thornwell Jacobs, the university president from 1915 to 1945. The school selected Roosevelt "in recognition of his high achievements in statesmanship, economics, and philanthropy." It honored the New York governor "as a Georgian, as a public official, and as an American." Oglethorpe initially planned a 1931 ceremony, but an illness of Sara Delano Roosevelt resulted in a delay, so the university instead honored a presidential candidate. Interest in the speech led officials at Oglethorpe to move the address from campus to the Fox Theater, a larger facility. The university had held the actual graduation ceremony a week earlier. Though closed due to the Depression and the bankruptcy of owner William Fox, the Fox Theater reopened for the occasion. A capacity crowd of over four thousand heard Roosevelt's remarks.

Six weeks before the address to Oglethorpe graduates, Roosevelt delivered his famous "forgotten man" radio address from Albany, New York. Sharply criticizing "trickle down" recovery programs, he demanded a program that "builds from the bottom up . . . that puts faith once more in the forgotten man at the bottom of the economic pyramid." His first significant follow-up on that theme came with this address at Oglethorpe. Members of the platform party in the photograph include, left to right, Dr. Thornwell Jacobs; Roosevelt; Governor Richard B. Russell Jr.; New York publisher Barron Collier; and Oglethorpe board member Edgar Watkins.

A CHANCE DISCUSSION with members of the media played a major role in the call for "bold persistent experimentation" presented to Oglethorpe graduates. Ernest K. Lindley, a journalist for the *New York Herald Tribune*, suggested much of the wording for the address. During a picnic at Dowdell's Knob near Warm Springs, three reporters traveling with Roosevelt kidded him about the lack of substantive comments since the "forgotten man" address. Roosevelt promptly challenged them to help him draft a better one if they did not like his speeches. Here, reporters, Roosevelt, Missy LeHand, and aides picnic by the covered pool at the Warm Springs Foundation. Staff called the group, which included the Secret Service, "the party." From left are Mary Hudson, who taught Eleanor Roosevelt how to swim; Louis Ruppel, a reporter for the *New York Daily News*; Lindley; James Kieran of the *New York Times*; Walter Brown of the *New York Times*; Missy LeHand; and FDR. In the back are Lou Weinberg, who worked in the business office at the institute, and Gus Gennerich.

Millions heard hope in these speeches, a hope they needed during desperate times. Others responded with less enthusiasm. The leftist tone of this address outraged longtime advisor Louis Howe. The *New York Times* criticized the blandness of the speech and the lack of specificity as Roosevelt said, "Try something." Nonetheless, in his last major speech before the Democratic National Convention, patrician Roosevelt clearly reached out to the "forgotten man." "Try something" harkened back to his first days at Warm Springs as he sought to improve his legs by trying different treatments.

STANDING BEHIND a "Roosevelt for President" poster, Roosevelt addresses the crowd, probably at a Warm Springs barbecue. A radio transmitter sits atop the podium allowing the address to be carried to even more Americans. Roosevelt became the first candidate and president to use radio extensively to reach the public. His "Fireside Chats" enabled his voice to enter the living rooms of millions of Americans, though none of those talks originated in Warm Springs.

ROOSEVELT AND RICHARD B. RUSSELL JR.
crossed paths numerous times during the 1930s. On May
13, 1932, Russell met the candidate, Lawrence Camp, and
other Georgia Democrats in Warm Springs to discuss the
political campaign. At the Democratic National Convention
in Chicago in the summer of 1932, Georgia governor Russell
made the seconding address to nominate Roosevelt.
Russell told the convention: "It has been the rare privilege of the people of Georgia to personally know Franklin
Delano Roosevelt—the man. . . . We recognize him not only
as a great Democrat and a great American but as the man of
the hour, best fitted to lead this nation in this time of trial."[84]

Roosevelt and Russell, who was seeking election to the
U.S. Senate, arrived in Warm Springs in October, two weeks
before the general election, to attend a meeting of the board
of the Warm Springs Foundation. Local newspapers estimated that the population of Warm Springs swelled to four
times its normal size as people welcomed the candidates
to town. The two traveled to Atlanta for a major campaign
appearance the next day. Russell won the seat and entered
the Senate as its youngest member. He strongly supported
farmers and agricultural programs, and his Senate votes
helped ensure passage of New Deal legislation.[85]

LARGE CROWDS greeted Roosevelt during his fall 1932 trip through Georgia. People lined the way through Warm Springs and awaited his arrival at the Little White House. Here the candidate pauses on a porch swing to examine his hat, which he had worn throughout the 1932 campaign, including visiting thirty-six of the forty-eight states.

Area supporters organized a reception in Greenville and a parade in Warm Springs to greet their favorite candidate. On October 28, 1932, the *Meriwether Vindicator* reported that Greenville welcomed him as "The Next President, Our Neighbor and Friend." In a stop at the Meriwether Inn, he told the crowd, "I am truly glad to be home. After November 8th, I am coming back down here and I can assure you we will have one of those Thanksgiving parties for which you and I are famous."[86] Then he apologized for his worn hat but added,

> You know, I have a superstition about hats and campaigns and I am going to go right on wearing it until the eighth of November . . . and then I am going to be alright anyway because as I drove up here I saw in the car in front of me old Fred Botts, with a silk hat, and that means instead of going to the expense of getting a silk hat before inauguration on March Fourth, why, I am just going to borrow Fred's.[87]

Roosevelt would not change hats in midcampaign. A former patient at Warm Springs who served as registrar and foundation manager, Botts had been known to wear a silk top hat on special occasions.

ROOSEVELT PAID A QUICK VISIT to Warm Springs on October 23, 1932. Institute staff guarded against allowing social events or interest from the press and the general public to take priority over medical routines. Officials knew that the foundation benefited from national exposure, but they did not want the privacy of patients invaded, nor did they want the general excitement to detract from the purpose of the center. In a letter to Arthur Carpenter in 1934, Roosevelt told him, "I wonder what you will do about the Press. I will back you one hundred per cent if you decide it is best not to put them on the campus."[88]

James L. Key, mayor of Atlanta, proclaimed Monday October 24, 1932, "Roosevelt Day." A crowd of 150,000 to 200,000 Georgians greeted the candidate as he rode in one of the largest parades held in Atlanta in the early twentieth century. *Atlanta Journal* headlines stated: "Tumultuous

Demonstration Greets Roosevelt Parade through City," while the *Constitution* called it "the greatest multitude ever assembled below the Mason and Dixon line."[89]

In reality, there was little need for Roosevelt to campaign in Georgia or the South since all signs indicated that he and the Democratic Party would win the southern vote. He might have used his time shaking hands in northern states such as Pennsylvania, where questions remained about voters' support. Roosevelt acknowledged this as he thanked Atlantans for their tremendous welcome and admitted that he did not need to come to Georgia to get votes. Instead he wanted to hear from Georgians, plus he could add in a trip to Warm Springs.

His visit may have been a way of saying thank you to the many people who had been supporting him since the 1920s. Frank Freidel declared, "Had it not been for Southern support, he would never have been nominated for President in 1932 and thus would have never reached the White House. . . . For better and for worse, the destinies of Franklin D. Roosevelt and the South were inextricably intermingled."[90]

Roosevelt told the *Atlanta Constitution* on October 25, 1932: "This is a day I shall never forget, I will see the eager faces and the lighted eyes of my fellow Georgians as long as I live. . . . I am deeply and everlastingly grateful to the people of this great state. I am proud to call it home." Roosevelt also knew that he would need assistance from southerners in Congress to translate New Deal campaign promises into reality. One photo here shows the front of the old Terminal Station in downtown Atlanta. The other shows Roosevelt and Richard B. Russell Jr. waving to the crowd from the back seat, while Hugh Howell, state Democratic chairman, sits between them. In the front seat are A. L. Belle Isle (driving), son James Roosevelt in the middle, and Atlanta Mayor James Key.

DURING POLITICAL CAMPAIGNS, candidates kiss and hold babies, shake hands, and speak to as many people as they can. At one stop in downtown Atlanta, Girls High School students Gladys Morrison and Kitty Frazier shook hands with the presidential contender as they walked beside the car and gave him a bouquet of flowers. (Girls High School became coeducational in 1947 and was renamed Roosevelt High School.) The route took Roosevelt from Peachtree Street to Little Five Points across Grant Park to Spring Street to the Biltmore Hotel and to the Atlanta Municipal Auditorium.

The *Atlanta Journal* declared: "[Roosevelt] rode in triumph Monday through the heart of Atlanta, receiving the acclaim of his fellow citizens, who regard him not only as an outstanding figure in American public life, but also as their neighbor and loyal friend."[91]

Frances Perkins, Roosevelt's secretary of labor, later said: "Campaigns always stimulated Roosevelt enormously. . . . He enjoyed the freedom and getting out among the people. . . . His personal relationship with crowds was on a warm, simple level of a friendly neighborly exchange of affection. . . . He learned to love people by trying to understand them and to find the common denominator between him and everyone with whom he had contact."[92]

Of course, not everyone loved him. Nan Pendergrast, later an active participant in the civil rights movement in Atlanta, opposed Roosevelt. "You know both of my parents . . . just frothed at the sight of this man. . . . So I think my first political act was in the seventh grade. He came to town, and I threw a wild onion at the car. It didn't hit it, but I thought about it." She and her family feared that his programs were "galloping socialism." Her father, president of Spring Bed Company, disliked Roosevelt even more after New Deal projects such as the National Recovery Administration came into being.[93]

DURING A BUSY DAY in Atlanta, Roosevelt addressed several audiences, including one at 9:30 a.m. outside Union Station. Roosevelt waved his hat triumphantly to greet the large crowd, while Atlanta mayor James Key sat to his right. The *Warm Springs Mirror* described Key as the "militant leader of anti-prohibition forces," and Roosevelt agreed that Prohibition should end. (Almost fourteen months later, Prohibition ended with passage of the Twenty-First Amendment.) Georgia governor Richard Russell and Senator John S. Cohen, along with representatives from eight other southern states, joined him at the podium.

A variety of activities filled the day, and several events had to be cancelled due to crowd size. Anna Roosevelt Dall planned to appear at a ceremony at the Henry W. Grady monument, which officials cancelled due to dense crowds. They thought it would take Roosevelt's daughter too long to get to the statue. Officials similarly cancelled ceremonies planned for City Hall and the State Capitol. Crowds slowed the governor's car to a stop during the parade, though police tried to keep the route clear of people.

HIGHLIGHTS OF THE Atlanta campaign included an appearance by Roosevelt at a luncheon in the Biltmore Hotel and an evening address at City Auditorium. Roosevelt was photographed speaking at the luncheon and with a group of women who had gathered to have their picture taken with him and Governor Russell. Others in the audience included U.S. senators and governors from most of the southern states and former secretary of state Breckinridge Long.

That evening, seven thousand people packed the Atlanta Municipal Auditorium, while thousands more gathered outside to listen to a broadcast of the proceedings. Others filled nearby Taft Hall to listen via speakers. WSB, WGST, and the Dixie Network of the Columbia Broadcasting System carried the address.

The governor of New York spoke for fifty-five minutes. He focused mainly on proposed agricultural reform and criticism of Herbert Hoover, the sitting president of the United States. Roosevelt asserted: "Mr. Hoover believes that farmers and workers must wait for general recovery. . . . I believe that we can restore prosperity here in this country by reestablishing the purchasing power of half of the people of the country; that when this gigantic market of 50 million people [farmers and their families] is able to purchase goods, industry will start to turn and the millions of men and women now walking the streets will be employed."[94]

The *Atlanta Constitution* reported that following the address Roosevelt requested that flowers used as table decorations be sent to the children's ward of Grady Hospital. The newspaper quoted him as saying: "Send them over to the sick kiddies, they'll enjoy them so much."[95] Roosevelt left Atlanta at 10:37 p.m. to continue his campaign in Raleigh, Richmond, and Baltimore.

WINFRED "TOBY" COOK (shown in this photograph), a six-year-old who rode 210 miles on a pony from Chula, Georgia, joined Roosevelt, Georgia senator John S. Cohen, and other political leaders at the podium during lunch at the Biltmore Hotel. Cook arrived the day before and led the parade through downtown Atlanta. A few days after returning home to Tift County, he led a parade of Hoover carts and "What Have Yous" through Tifton. The *Tifton Gazette* described Hoover carts by comparing them to "Depression Chariots." The carts and what have yous were generally the remains of old cars, wagons, or other carts pulled by a mule, reflecting the fact that the owners of the automobile could not afford gasoline during the Depression. The Tifton parade was a highlight of weekend festivities designed by the local board of trade to "'poke some fun' at Old Man Depression."[96]

A few months later, the then seven-year-old rode ponies 811 miles to participate in the inaugural parade in Washington, D.C. The president saluted as Toby passed the reviewing stand. Traveling with his father and two farmhands, Toby rode in five-mile relays on three ponies, Billy, Jim, and Pet, and took fifteen days to get to the capital. While traveling through Virginia, he and his favorite pony, Billy, got caught in road construction. An automobile hit the pony and threw them over a fence. The pony had to be euthanized. The *Tifton Gazette* reported on March 3, 1933: "Toby's father, J. D. Cook, Jr., accepted the large sedan that struck the pony in settlement for the damages." After his arrival, Toby received celebrity treatment, spoke on national radio shows, and met political leaders and screen stars such as Kate Smith, Buffalo Bill Jr., and Amos 'n' Andy. The group rode home in the car that his father had driven to Washington, while the ponies rode in a horse van. (Tragically, Toby Cook's life was cut short during World War II. He volunteered for service in the U.S. Marine Corps and was killed at Iwo Jima in 1945.)[97]

Young Cook's antics personified the joy of the state in having one of its own in the White House. Citizens saw Democrat Roosevelt as the answer to their economic problems. Historians have noted that in such tough economic conditions, Roosevelt appeared to many Georgians as almost Christlike. Roosevelt became a symbol of hope.[98]

FRANKLIN ROOSEVELT
enjoys a quiet talk with his daughter, Anna Dall, in front of a fire at the Little White House during his November–December 1932 visit. A month earlier, Roosevelt had won election as president of the United States by a landslide. Georgia voted fifteen to one for its adopted son. While in Warm Springs, Roosevelt and his daughter joined patients for the traditional Founders' Day Dinner on Thanksgiving Day. Southern leaders, including Senators John H. Bankhead of Alabama and Joseph T. Robinson of Arkansas, senator-elect Richard B. Russell Jr., governor-elect Eugene Talmadge, members of the Georgia Bicentennial Commission, and key advisors visited during this "vacation."

ROOSEVELT LOVED MUSIC and often invited groups to play during his stays at Warm Springs. Musicians from surrounding counties gathered in January 1933 to serenade the president-elect. Roosevelt and daughter Anna joined them on the lawn for one photo. In another photo, with members of the press and other men gathered around Roosevelt, the musicians are (left to right) Lester Riggins, Bun Wright of Upson County, Bud Saylor, Roosevelt, Tom Millens, Rufus Millens, and Ferrell Garrard. The men included farmers who played together often even though several did not read sheet music.

Vernon Lofton stated: "I remember being down at Mr. Waddell's one day. . . . They were all sitting on the porch playing music and he [Roosevelt] was in his Plymouth with the top let back. . . . He listened to them play music. . . . Mr. Bun Wright was his favorite musician. He was a fiddler. Mr. Roosevelt really enjoyed it."[99]

Reubin Bridges added that Mr. Roosevelt told the group: "'I want to hear some good old South music, down South music.' We started playing 'Home on the Range.' Musical instruments included fiddles, banjo, guitar, and mandolin. After we played, he said pass the gourd around. One of them reached down there and got the gourd with moonshine in it. He [Roosevelt] got some and laughed and talked and after a while started playing some of our good old Southern music again. We had a real ball there that day."[100]

Martin Gibson lived in the Cove. He recalled that "Old Man Waddell" offered Roosevelt some peach brandy. "I think Mr. Waddell asked him if he would have a drink and he said, 'yes, bring it out.' Of course, he was sitting in his car. He [Waddell] brought it out in a little fruit jar. Why it all happened like that I can't figure out. It seemed to me that he would have brought a glass out but he didn't. He [Roosevelt] swallowed that peach brandy out of that fruit jar . . . [and] handed it back to him."[101]

A young boy when his father worked as resident trustee of the Warm Springs Foundation, Robert Carpenter reflected that "Roosevelt was such a good sport. . . . He ate their possum. . . . He would go up there and drink their corn liquor."[102]

ON DECEMBER 6, 1932, Eleanor, Franklin, and Anna Roosevelt, along with bodyguard Gus Gennerich, prepare to depart for New York State. Anna holds the book *Epic America*, her reading material for the long train ride. Eleanor probably had knitting in her bag to pass the travel time. Franklin, Eleanor, Henry Morgenthau, and others visited again from January 24 to February 4, 1933. Morgenthau spoke to a meeting of the Meriwether County Welfare Board, and Eleanor told Willie Vie Dowdy, home improvement specialist in extension work for the University System of Georgia, about the social value of handicraft and its use by New York State 4-H Clubs.

Despite her apparent gaiety that day, Eleanor Roosevelt spent considerably less time in Georgia than her husband. Mrs. Lee Rowe of Meriwether County, who with her husband supplied eggs and chickens to Roosevelt during his earliest visits, remembered that Eleanor visited Warm Springs "once in a while," but remarked, "I never did see her unless she made a speech around the school house or somewhere."[103]

Eleanor Roosevelt primarily came for major foundation functions or political events. She never really felt comfortable in Warm Springs. Perhaps she considered it to be Franklin's home but not hers. She spent many years between 1918 and her death in 1962 seeking to improve the human condition but admitted: "It was a disappointment to me to find that for many, many people, life in the South was hard and poor and ugly, just as it is in parts of the North. Even though I realized how greatly many people benefitted from the place, I never really enjoyed living in Warm Springs as much as my husband did."[104]

Warm Springs may have been too isolated for Mrs. Roosevelt, and she also did not approve of the treatment of blacks in the South. Her public comments and actions about race tended to focus on issues such as lynchings. She coordinated meetings between Roosevelt and NAACP leader Walter White in 1934 to discuss anti-lynching legislation.

Mrs. Roosevelt offered a different view of Warm Springs in 1934 when, as first lady, she wrote about the foundation: "It is a joy to go back there year after year and see the improvements which have gradually come about and the efficient organization where patients can receive the very best of care. The part of it which has always interested me is the assistance which is rendered to people who cannot afford to pay full price for their care. The Patients Aid Fund is raised every year, and so far it has never been possible to raise enough to meet the needs of the people throughout the country who are suffering from the effects of this disease."[105]

MEMBERS OF HIS FAMILY
—wife Eleanor, daughter Anna, or one of his sons—often accompanied Roosevelt on campaign trips. Here Roosevelt waves his hat while Eleanor and Anna smile at the crowd in a triumphant postcampaign visit to Warm Springs to rest, recuperate, and plan for the new administration. Local residents enthusiastically greeted the Roosevelts on their first trip back to the area following his election as president of the United States.

CHAPTER 4

Leading the Nation

MERIWETHER COUNTY strongly supported Roosevelt in presidential elections. In 1925, both *Vindicator* editor Henry H. Revill and Warm Springs manager Tom Loyless mentioned him as a possible candidate for president. County residents organized the first Roosevelt for President Club in November 1930. In the March 1932 Democratic primary, Warm Springs residents cast 213 votes for Roosevelt and one for the opposition. Over two thousand Meriwether County voters supported their neighbor, while fifteen voted for proxy candidate Speaker of the House John N. Garner.[1]

In the general election in November, Roosevelt solidly won election as president of the United States, carrying all but six states. Residents of Meriwether County voted overwhelming in favor of their part-time resident, though not unanimously as requested by local newspaper editors. They gave Roosevelt 2,604 votes compared to 53 for Hoover. Statewide, Georgians gave their adopted son a 92 percent majority compared to a national figure of 59 percent.[2]

In 1936, Roosevelt lost some support in Meriwether County as Alf Landon received 138 votes compared to his 2,438 votes. The *Meriwether Vindicator* proclaimed in a long headline: "President Roosevelt Swept the United Sates like a Georgia Cyclone. Forty-Six States in His Column by Large Majorities. Landon Carried Only the States of Maine and Vermont. Greatest Victory Ever Won." Warm Springs residents cast 210 votes for their part-time neighbor and 14 for Landon.[3]

In July 1938, some residents of Meriwether County already wanted Roosevelt to stay in office. John Lear of the Associated Press interviewed Revill, who thought Roosevelt might have to run for a third term in 1940. He added: "He'll have to run again if he can't find someone else who can carry on his policies. If he didn't run and didn't find someone strong enough to carry on what he has begun we would lose everything we have gained during his administration." The story added that there was no indication whether Roosevelt was considering such a precedent-setting move.[4] (Other newspaper editors in the area were not as enthusiastic about a possible third term. The *LaGrange Daily News* stated that Roosevelt should step aside for the sake of American democracy and patriotism, no matter how much his followers insisted that he seek a third term.)

By 1940, the threat of war had become more real. Following a pattern similar to that in 1936, Meriwether voted for Roosevelt 2,726 to 174 votes for Willkie and 8 for the Prohibition candidate. Warm Springs cast 226 out of 236 votes for Roosevelt. In 1944, when Roosevelt won his fourth term in office, Meriwether County cast 2,187 votes for Roosevelt, 181 for Dewey, and 7 for the Independent Democratic candidate. Warm Springs cast 164 votes for the president, 13 for the Republican, and 3 for the Independent Democratic candidate.[5]

WHILE VISITING WARM SPRINGS, Roosevelt carried on the business of his offices. Mail dispatches arrived via Fort Benning, allowing him to keep up with correspondence and news. He often worked on upcoming speeches. Government leaders from throughout the United States and foreign countries frequently visited him at Warm Springs. Gathered on the porch at the Little White House in this November 28, 1933, photograph are secretary of agriculture Henry A. Wallace (seated) and Eugene Vidal, director of Aeronautics, Department of Commerce. Wallace served as vice president from 1941 to 1945 during Roosevelt's third term in office. In describing the group, the *Warm Springs Mirror* noted that Vidal had been an All-American quarterback during his years at West Point.

During the trip, Vidal probably visited the airfield at Warm Springs. On May 15, 1932, area residents had dedicated the airport in honor of the New York chief executive. Several thousand people attended the ceremony and watched an exhibition of army planes from Fort Benning and army reserve pilots from Candler Field in Atlanta, including an aerial circus, parachute jumping, and other activities. In his dedicatory address, Roosevelt traced transportation developments over the centuries and activities at Warm Springs. He mentioned, as he often did, the fact that the springs had long been a destination since the days when they were a healing sanctuary for Indian warriors. He added, "I too have found peace at Warm Springs."[6] The airfield was designed for the convenience of visiting dignitaries, polio patients and their parents, and, as the *Warm Springs Advertiser* stated on May 23, 1931, "for use by visiting birdmen who may wish to stop over here." Many expected Roosevelt to use the field, though he did not like to fly and preferred to journey by train or car. He declared he might make use of the field "when time saving [was] expedient," but he never did. The airport was a project of the Civil Works Administration, a New Deal agency designed to create jobs.

MARTHA BERRY, a pioneer educator in Georgia and founder of Berry College near Rome, visited Warm Springs in January 1933. She and the president-elect are shown chatting on the porch of the Little White House in this photo. In 1902, she established her first school, a boarding school for boys. Her schools for boys and girls soon became models throughout the world for how poor children in rural areas could be educated. Roosevelt expressed admiration for Berry's work and pledged his support. The day of her visit she spoke to patients about her struggles to establish a school for poor mountain children.

Also visiting Warm Springs at the time was Sara Delano Roosevelt, Franklin's mother. She visited only a few times, though she returned ten months later that year to celebrate Georgia's bicentennial. She had first visited Warm Springs in September 1926, soon after her son purchased the property. Sara Roosevelt and Martha Berry were friends, having met at receptions in New York when Berry was fund-raising for her schools. She visited Berry during this trip and mentioned her admiration of Berry to an audience in Savannah. Republican presidents Theodore Roosevelt and Calvin Coolidge and businessmen like Henry Ford visited the Berry School, but Democrat Franklin Roosevelt never scheduled a visit, despite Berry's frequent requests.[7]

THE FIRST PRESIDENTIAL INAUGURATION in 1933 of Georgia's favorite son became a major event for his friends. Judge Henry Revill, chair of the Meriwether County Roosevelt for President Club, announced that a special train would run from Warm Springs to Washington, D.C., for the March 4 event. Supporters from around the state, including fiddlers from the Cove, businessmen, and political leaders, traveled to the capital on the "Warm Springs Special." Twenty-six members of Troup FDR from Manchester represented the Boy Scouts of America in the inaugural parade. In the mid-1920s, Roosevelt served as chairman of the Boy Scouts of Greater New York, helped raise funds for their activities, and always supported scouting. Bill Trotter, one of the scouts, remembered marching in the parade as "cold but exciting." He also recalled that people contributed money to send the scouts to Washington in the midst of the Depression. At the end of the trip, the scouts gave the remaining $2.50 to the building fund of Georgia Hall at the foundation.[8] The Franklin D. Roosevelt Boy Scout troop gathered to have an official photograph taken and, in a less formal scene, to greet the new president.

The Inaugural Committee
requests the honor of the presence of
Mr. and Mrs. Arthur Carpenter
to attend and participate in the Inauguration of

Franklin Delano Roosevelt
as President of the United States of America
and

John Nance Garner
as Vice President of the United States of America
on Saturday the fourth of March
one thousand nine hundred and thirty-three
in the City of Washington

Please reply to Ray Baker
Chairman Committee on Reception of Governors of States
Special Distinguished Guests
Washington Building Washington, D.C.

Cary T. Grayson
Chairman, Inaugural Committee

MAIL BOXES brought delight to Warm Springs residents when they held invitations to attend the inauguration of Roosevelt as president of the United States. Forty-two patients and staff from the Warm Springs Foundation comprised a special group at the inauguration. Representing fifteen states and the Philippine Islands, they rode the Warm Springs Special. L. B. Merwin reported on the trip in the *Bloomington (Illinois) Pantagraph*: "I doubt if any group gathering there . . . will attract a modicum of the throng's attention as does this band of loyal friends and fellow sufferes [*sic*] from the dread malady of infantile paralysis . . . I have yet to detect a feeling among them of discouragement or despondence. On the contrary, they seem unusually optimistic in this period of depression; more so than the average citizen one meets in travel or at home. Our new President has been an inspiration to every person in the colony."[9] Roosevelt wrote his acceptance himself while at his home in Hyde Park on February 27, 1933, acknowledging that great challenges lay ahead.

A member of the Warm Springs delegation, Fred Botts, wrote Missy LeHand: "In Washington, we had but to say we were from Warm Springs and a path would open through the crowd and doors swing wide for our crutches." Contingents of Georgians and Warm Springs residents attended each of Roosevelt's inaugurals.[10]

> We face the arduous days that lie before us in the warm courage of national unity; with the clear consciousness of seeking old and precious moral values; with the clean satisfaction that comes from the stern performance of duty by old and young alike. We aim at the assurance of a rounded and permanent national life.
>
> In this dedication of a nation we humbly ask the blessing ~~and the guidance~~ of God. May he protect each and every one of us. May he guide me in the days to come.
>
> Franklin D. Roosevelt

GEORGIA GOVERNOR Eugene Talmadge had this special train car for the trip to Washington, D.C., in March. The governor-elect and the president were good friends at this point. The state capped off festivities for the "Georgia Bicentennial Celebration 1733–1933" with President's Day in Savannah on November 18, 1933. A twenty-one-gun salute greeted Roosevelt on his arrival and departure from Municipal Stadium. Roosevelt served as honorary chairman of the Georgia Bicentennial Commission, while Governor Talmadge was its president. In October, the governor had declared that this address would be "the crowning event of the Celebration." He added: "We are very proud of the history of Georgia, and also that the President of our country is the great friend of Georgia and calls it his second home." Between thirty-five thousand and forty thousand people from throughout coastal Georgia and South Carolina greeted Roosevelt on his first trip to Georgia as president of the United States. Local newspapers declared that this was the biggest day in south Georgia in many years, asserting, "All Georgia roads will lead to Savannah this morning."

Roosevelt began his talk by recognizing that Georgia and its people meant much to his family. He acknowledged the crowds by declaring:

> I am happy in the thought that it has been a change for the better; that I have come back to see smiles replacing gloom, to see hope replacing despair, and to see faith restored to its rightful place. . . . While we are celebrating the planting of the colony of Georgia, we remember that if the early settlers had been content to remain on the coast, there would have been no Georgia today. It was the spirit of moving forward that led to the exploration of the great domain of piedmont and the mountains that drove the western border of the colony to the very banks of the Mississippi River itself.

He also mentioned that he looked forward to the upcoming Thanksgiving holiday at the Warm Springs Institute. He encouraged citizens to remember those less fortunate than themselves and ended by proclaiming: "I am counting on the individual citizen and his inherent character to continue with me on our march of progress."[11] Bill Harris in the *Savannah Morning News* declared that those at the stadium were "enraptured almost to immobility by the magnetic personality of the man."[12]

F. BASIL ABRAMS, a photographer for the *Savannah Evening Press*, took this photo of President Roosevelt addressing the crowd at Municipal Stadium in Savannah. On the back of the photograph someone wrote: "Base got arrested snapping this because he got too near his royal highness and it cost 5 rocks fine." The meaning of this message remains unclear since the photograph shows nothing inflammatory. Abrams might have upset Secret Service agents by getting too close to the president, or perhaps they thought that he had photographed Roosevelt's leg braces or his difficulty walking. In general, photographers respected Roosevelt's privacy and did not depict his disability—though this may not have always been their first choice.

A PRESIDENTIAL PARADE followed the Municipal Stadium address and concluded with a reception at the DeSoto Hilton. Savannah mayor Thomas Gamble, former city editor for the *Savannah Evening Press*, rode between the president and his mother, Sara Delano Roosevelt. This was Franklin's second visit to the city, which he had briefly visited in 1922. Both Roosevelts admired the beauty of the area and its architecture. As they traveled along Bull Street between Forsyth Park and Victory Drive, Mrs. Roosevelt assured them that she had never seen a more beautiful street and told reporters that "the miles of happy faces were like a great physical and spiritual tonic" for her son.[13]

Georgia governor Eugene Talmadge rode in the front seat. Following the visit to Savannah, Talmadge accompanied the president through Cordele and Fitzgerald to Warm Springs for a weekend stay. The *Savannah Morning News* reported: "The President . . . has taken a distinct liking for the vigorous Georgia Governor. . . . It is anticipated that the talks between the President and the Governor will result in even closer relations between the President and his adopted state of Georgia."[14] Instead, the trip likely marked the high point of their relationship. Both men were Democrats, but their differences became obvious during the next year. Roosevelt embraced liberalism, while Talmadge was a much more conservative "populist."

In his 1935 inaugural speech as governor of Georgia, Talmadge stated: "The only way I know a government can help the people is to stay out of business, and be a fair referee between the people and let its citizens do the business, and then just take as little toll out of their property as you can for government." In May 1935, over one thousand residents of Meriwether County signed a petition endorsing the president and condemning Governor Talmadge for his attacks on the president. After pronouncing Roosevelt's Social Security plan to be a combination of the worst features of communism and socialism, Talmadge stayed at his farm in Telfair County rather than be in Atlanta on November 29, 1935, when thousands greeted the president at the Georgia School of Technology (later called Georgia Institute of Technology). Talmadge told his secretaries: "I am spending the day on my Telfair County farm hunting and farming—hunting something to plant that there's not any processing tax on." In January 1936, Talmadge went further by being the only member of the Democratic National Committee to vote no on a resolution endorsing the Roosevelt administration. Georgians feared that these personal differences would hurt the state.[15]

A FEW DAYS BEFORE the Georgia Bicentennial Celebration in Savannah, citizens in Fitzgerald and Cordele began receiving reports that the president might visit as he traveled from Savannah to Warm Springs on the Atlantic, Birmingham and Coast (AB&C) rail line. The *Fitzgerald Herald* reported on November 17: "The possibility of President Roosevelt spending five minutes or more in the city grows stronger. . . . No President has ever been in this section of Georgia. . . . This is the only chance thousands will ever have to see and hear our President." Governor Talmadge extended the invitation to the president on behalf of citizens of the towns.

On November 19, between four thousand and ten thousand people gathered around the passenger train station in the seat of Ben Hill County as the photograph here shows. In July, Fitzgerald had been recognized as the first city in the nation to officially pledge cooperation with the president's economic recovery plans as political, business, and civic leaders signaled their support for the National Recovery Act. Talmadge welcomed the crowd by stating: "We all want to hear the President speak—but there is one thing I want to say, that we have got a real President who is for the average little man and little woman in this country." Sara Delano Roosevelt then greeted the crowd, followed by her son, who told the group: "I see a whole lot more smiles on people's faces than I did a year ago. . . . It gives me pleasure to assure you that we continue to bring to the masses of people the relief to which they have honored me with their votes."[16]

A few miles away, thousands more gathered at the train station in Cordele. Roosevelt had twice visited with Crisp County delegations concerned about the development of the local hydroelectric plant. The president assured the crowd of how impressed he had been with the county leaders. He told them, "In various parts of the United States I have held Crisp County as one of the fine examples of good American progressive citizenship." According to the *Cordele Dispatch*, "The colored population, too, was very much interested in getting a glimpse of Mr. Roosevelt. It was indeed a momentous occasion. Our beloved chief executive who is the center of interest everywhere—all over the world—seemed delighted to be among us. His extremely friendly personality . . . was fully verified Saturday when Mr. Roosevelt appeared on the platform of his coach."[17]

NOVEMBER 1933 provided the first opportunity for most locals at Warm Springs to greet their new president. Roosevelt arrived in time to share Thanksgiving dinner with patients at the Warm Springs Foundation. His car sits at the end of the ramp as Secret Service agents keep crowds at arm's length and prevent them from jostling the ramp. Their caution may have been heightened due to an assassination attempt on Roosevelt in Miami eight months earlier. Although Roosevelt escaped unscathed, Chicago mayor Anton J. Cermak, who happened to be visiting south Florida, took a bullet and died a short time later. Roosevelt spoke briefly, telling the crowd: "May I thank you all. I don't have to say that it comes from the bottom of my heart, because you know that it does. I am awfully glad to be back home again with my neighbors in Meriwether County and Warm Springs."[18]

By the time the president's train reached Warm Springs, a large crowd, often including Boy Scouts, would be on hand to greet him. Bands such as the Manchester "Y" Fife and Drum Corps would play. Roosevelt would wave and shake hands before he motored by the foundation and then to his home.

In an undated letter, Dr. Mike Hoke, medical director at Warm Springs from 1927 to 1935, wrote the president just after his arrival. "Heartfelt greetings from us all here! Some of us 'old timers' did not meet you at the train for the very simple reason that the Foundation greeting was arranged to occur at Georgia Hall. Of course, the heart of this place pulses with warmth for you and yours. . . . Have a good time; don't let us bother you and at such time as it is convenient we would love to come up and shake hands."[19]

NATIONAL EVENTS touched Georgians more closely when Roosevelt vacationed in the state. On the day the president left for Savannah in November 1933, the United States formally recognized Soviet Russia. Roosevelt stated, "I believe that through the resumption of normal relations the prospects of peace over all the world are greatly strengthened."[20] The day after he reached Warm Springs, he met with Sumner Welles (shown with Roosevelt in the photo), who had just arrived from Havana. After being attacked by Cuban students, Welles had requested this conference with Roosevelt. A series of revolts threatened American commercial interests in Cuba. Welles, U.S. ambassador to Cuba and a fellow Groton alumnus, advocated limited intervention in the situation, but Roosevelt and Secretary of State Cordell Hull refused. The United States wanted Cuba to establish a more stable government. On November 23, Roosevelt issued a proclamation stating that any island government must have the support of the people and demonstrated stability before the Good Neighbor Policy could be extended. After returning briefly to Cuba, Welles rejoined the administration in Washington, D.C., as assistant secretary of state concerned with Latin American affairs.

Grace Tully, a longtime assistant and a frequent visitor to Warm Springs, stated: "The trait which I believe Roosevelt possessed in a more generous degree that most people—and it was a trait the country was to sense on his inauguration day—was a will to assume pressing responsibility for events, and a will to make decisions regarding them."[21]

A RARE PHOTO of Roosevelt standing with his cane was probably taken in Warm Springs. Many local people had gathered to see their famous neighbor. Another shows Roosevelt walking near the train with assistance from Gus Gennerich, his longtime bodyguard and friend. Gennerich usually accompanied Roosevelt to Warm Springs. His sudden death in November 1936, while on a presidential trip to Buenos Aires, saddened many at the foundation. The *Warm Springs Mirror* noted that he was the "beloved favorite of the poliomyelitis patients at the Foundation, with the exception of the President, himself."[22]

Another Roosevelt train trip led Downing Musgrove to have sad memories of the president. Musgrove served as executive secretary to Georgia governor E. D. Rivers from 1937 to 1940. He met many national political leaders, including House Speaker John H. Bankhead and Harry Hopkins, when he transported them from Terminal Station in Atlanta to the governor's office and on to the Little White House. The governor of Tennessee invited Rivers and Musgrove to join Roosevelt on September 2, 1940, for the dedication of Chickamauga Dam in Chattanooga.

When they arrived at the depot, they drove by the train. Musgrove remembered:

> I'm sorry that they let us do it . . . to see him being unloaded from that train, go down those narrow steps and to that automobile—he was in braces; and he was just as brave as he could be, but you could tell that everything that he did, he was in intense pain until he was able to get into the car and sit down. And then, as soon as he got out of that, he just lightened up again; and the whole world would light up with him. . . . But just to watch him and know that every time he moved, he had to go through that, it was pretty saddening.[23]

IN DECEMBER 1933, the president joined Mayor Sam Killian for a flag raising in the town's business district. Roosevelt reminisced about his first visit nine years earlier and pledged that his family intended to see that a United States flag always flew over town. Eleanor Roosevelt joined them for the occasion, having just finished addressing the Fourth District Woman's Club Convention held in Warm Springs. The theme of that meeting was "We Do Our Part," as the convention "planned to bring the club women the inspiration and quickening needed in the present readjustment." Members of the Roosevelt Boy Scout Drum and Bugle Corps, the Georgia Military Academy band, and others joined in the flag raising. The president donated the regulation army flag at the request of the Woman's Club.[24]

ROOSEVELT AND ADVISORS work amid the pines at the Little White House on a spring day. Henry Morgenthau Jr., an old friend from Hyde Park, is shown on the left. A member of the brain trust that counseled Roosevelt during his 1932 presidential campaign, Morgenthau later served as secretary of the treasury. An unidentified man stands on the right. Visits to Warm Springs by advisors and members of the cabinet were common. In December 1934, Morgenthau; James Farley, postmaster general; Undersecretary of Agriculture Rexford G. Tugwell; Secretary of the Interior Harold Ickes; Federal Relief administrator Harry L. Hopkins; Charles Michaelson, publicity director for the Democratic National Convention; and Frank Walker, one time head of the president's national executive council, all traveled from Warm Springs to the nation's capital aboard the "Presidential Special" railcar.[25]

THE PEOPLE OF SOUTH GEORGIA generally supported Roosevelt, though they saw less of him than others in the state and many opposed his farming programs. Born in 1924, the same year Roosevelt "discovered" Warm Springs, future president Jimmy Carter was one such man. With him in the photograph are his father, James Earl Carter Sr., and his sisters Gloria (left) and Ruth.

Carter grew up in Plains, Georgia, about seventy miles from Warm Springs. Like most Americans alive during the Depression, he experienced the impact of Roosevelt's programs. He once described his father's peripheral role in the New Deal. "Daddy was one of the first directors of the Sumter Electric Membership Corporation, and he became active in protecting the REA system. This was his first entrée into state and therefore national politics. He would go to Washington to lobby along with other farmers to protect the REA system, and he would go to national conventions of the REA. . . . This was when I was fourteen which was 1938 or so."[26]

Like many, Carter's father did not support all New Deal programs. Carter said: "What my father objected to was that the government required farmers to plow up cotton and to kill hogs and to waste the crops in that way. Daddy thought it was an unwarranted intrusion into his own personal farm affairs by the federal government." James Carter Sr. liked having electricity in his house, however, and he was very supportive of the REA, a program created by Roosevelt. Yet he also liked Walter George, resented Roosevelt's efforts in 1938 to defeat George, and did not think the federal government should get involved in telling farmers which crops to plant.[27]

Robert Copeland, an African American, worked on Roosevelt's farm for many years. He stated that "cotton was so cheap the farmer wasn't getting anything out of it. So FDR said you could only plant so much allotment. He let poor folks make up mattresses and they got the mattress free. Kind of a trade-off."[28]

ESTABLISHED as a Depression-era program to put young men who needed jobs to work in programs improving the environment and creating parks, the Civilian Conservation Corps benefited the Pine Mountain area. A camp was established in 1933 atop Pine Mountain but soon moved to Warm Springs to be near water and supplies. The CCC built a tavern that rented rooms, a pool, and several other buildings. The National Park Service designed the park buildings that the CCC built. The tavern opened in 1938, and the Georgia Department of Natural Resources has managed the site since 1934. The state called the site Pine Mountain State Park and later renamed it FDR State Park. Though the CCC ceased to exist in the late 1930s, the tavern (shown in the photo), with its fieldstone exterior and interior, is still in use as the visitors center for the FDR State Park. Liberty Bell Pool is still used each summer.[29]

Ruth Stevens reports that Roosevelt frequently checked on the progress of the CCC. On one occasion, he told the corps workers: "Boys, you remember that when we took over the reins of government, I said that I didn't expect to make a hit every time I went to bat, but I would be in there swinging at them. Well, fellows, I can say with a great deal of pride, that I made a four-base hit here."[30] Roosevelt seldom used sports metaphors when giving talks but chose to do so in addressing these young men. On December 7, 1935, he recognized the fact that the Warm Springs camp had been operating as long as any camp in the United States. "I have seen the work that this camp and the Chipley Camp has performed in the last couple of years. You are rendering a real service, not only to this community but to this part of the State and the whole State. It is permanent work, it is work that is going to be useful for a good many generations to come." As he left that day, Roosevelt displayed his usual interest in all people by asking to be introduced to the camp cooks because "they [were] the most important people in the Camp."[31]

ELEANOR ROOSEVELT sometimes appeared at political events with Franklin and usually attended the Founder's Day Dinners each Thanksgiving, but she seldom stayed the duration of his visits. She occasionally visited the Peach State without her husband to make speeches, such as those she gave at Valdosta, Covington, Monroe, and Atlanta. On at least one occasion, she stayed at Warm Springs accompanied only by her close friend, pioneering female journalist Lorena Hickok.[32] Eleanor flew to Georgia for the meeting while Hickok was on a tour of the South, reporting to Harry Hopkins on economic conditions. They exchanged thousands of letters over the years and developed a possibly intimate relationship. They stayed at McCarthy Cottage at Warm Springs because the Little White House was occupied. Eleanor Roosevelt stands between two unidentified women; Hickock is on the far right.

ROOSEVELT HAD less free time in Warm Springs after becoming president, but he still enjoyed two of his favorite pastimes there: going for rides in the countryside and having picnics. For one picnic, Cason Callaway and his family gathered with Roosevelt and his advisors at the Callaways' Blue Springs home near Hamilton. Cason Callaway sat left of Roosevelt; on the right were Virginia (Jinks) Callaway, an unidentified man, and Howard H. "Bo" Callaway. Bo and Jinks were also pictured with Roosevelt in another photo. Bo remembered guests being warned in advance that politics and special pleadings to the president were forbidden. The Callaways wanted their friend the president to be able to relax. Roosevelt even had a signal—when he loudly whispered, "Hep, hep," others were to break out in lively singing.[33]

In his 1965 publication about his father, Bo states that Cason and Roosevelt "disagreed fundamentally on all the fundamentals but as a man and friend, [his] father genuinely loved FDR." Bo Callaway later entered politics, and in 1968 he became the only Georgian to win the popular vote but not become governor when he failed to win the majority of votes, and the Georgia legislature then decided the issue. The Democratic legislature chose the Democratic nominee, Lester Maddox, as governor of Georgia. Callaway, a Republican, went on to serve as secretary of state under President Gerald Ford and played an active role in the party.[34]

157

ROOSEVELT'S INNER CIRCLE of advisors included his "brain trust," cabinet members, and close friends, but counted few Georgians as members. Historian Frank Freidel explains the relationship between Roosevelt and southern politicians: "For their part, the Southern politicians admired Roosevelt for his strenuous efforts to learn to walk again, and were inspired by his labors to build Warm Springs into a polio therapy center. They could not fail to be flattered by the warm attention he bestowed upon them, the way he fell into their honorific, oratorical habits, and the zest with which he played with them. He greeted their jokes with loud, hearty laughter; he shared their banter."[35]

Senators Richard B. Russell Jr. and Walter F. George and Governor E. D. Rivers supported Roosevelt and his programs to varying degrees. Russell supported some New Deal measures and saw the president several times a year. He voted against a New Deal measure to legalize and tax beer and often opposed the president on labor matters. He refused to participate in efforts to oust Walter George from the Senate in the 1938 election, even though Lawrence Camp, Roosevelt's candidate, had been chairman of the State Executive Committee under Russell. Roosevelt barely spoke to Russell for the next two years.

George faithfully attended Roosevelt's public appearances in Georgia but often voted against liberal New Deal measures, including efforts to add members to the Supreme Court. Rivers, first elected to statewide office in 1936, strongly supported Roosevelt throughout his career and ran on his own "Little New Deal" platform. Other legislative and local political leaders in Georgia, where the Democratic Party dominated elections, had similar relationships with Roosevelt.

They liked him, often voted with him, but did not always agree with his policies. L. W. "Chip" Robert served as assistant secretary of the treasury, but Cason Callaway declined to serve in Roosevelt's subcabinet.

Few Georgians opposed Roosevelt as strongly as Eugene Talmadge. By 1935, the governor considered him to be a great detriment to the nation and refused to make appearances with him. Showing a streak of cruelty, Talmadge told the *New York Times* and the *Atlanta Constitution* on April 19, 1935, that Roosevelt was an "extreme Radical" and snipped: "The greatest calamity to this country is that President Roosevelt can't walk around and hunt up people to talk to. The only voices to reach his wheelchair were the cries of the 'gimme crowd.'" He added that the next president would be someone who could work long hours in the sun and walk a two-by-four plank too.

On November 27, 1935, President and Mrs. Roosevelt combined a vacation at Warm Springs with a political visit, which he insisted on calling a "Welcome Home" meeting. A day after the traditional Thanksgiving dinner, huge crowds greeted the presidential motorcade in Atlanta and heard a speech at Grant Field. Committees in towns and counties across Georgia organized motorcades to travel to Atlanta to greet the president. Judson J. Milam, chairman of the Troup County delegation, reported that Atlanta police had assured him that "everyone in the delegations from outside Atlanta ha[d] been promised a place to park!" An even larger audience heard Roosevelt's words via radio broadcast over two nationwide networks.[36]

The *Atlanta Journal* summed up the outpouring of support: "It is more than a tribute of party allegiance and popular enthusiasm. It is the proud and grateful acknowledgement of . . . the most effectual friend this state and region had had in the White House since the war of the eighteen-sixties."[37]

During the motorcade, the Roosevelts sat next to each other, providing the press with a rare photographic opportunity. Seated next to Mrs. Roosevelt is Georgia senator Walter F. George, while his colleague Richard B. Russell Jr. occupies the front seat. Governors from Alabama, South Carolina, and Florida plus representatives from across the South participated, but Georgia governor Eugene Talmadge stayed home in Telfair County, though someone hung a likeness of him, complete with red suspenders, in effigy on the state capitol grounds, clearly visible to visitors.[38]

A CROWD of approximately fifty thousand greeted the president at Grant Field on the campus of the Georgia School of Technology. During the weekend, Roosevelt dedicated the new Techwood housing project, located near the school's campus. Georgia senators Richard Russell and Walter George, members of Congress, and others joined Roosevelt at the podium. Russell served as master of ceremonies, while George introduced the president. Roosevelt and supporters had decided earlier in the fall that a major public event that excluded the governor would quiet Talmadge. As Harlee Branch, an employee of the postmaster general, told Missy LeHand: "Many loyal supporters of the President, who are outraged at the daily attacks which Talmadge has been making against the President for weeks, feel that it would be not only unfortunate but very harmful, if Talmadge were permitted to participate in the welcome to the President."[39]

Roosevelt agreed that it would be best not to give the governor another chance to publicly criticize him. He asked Branch in a memo: "Can you get confidential word to the committee that I prefer not to be received in any way by any persons other than the Senators and Congressmen?" The visit met their expectations as huge crowds greeted the president at his "other home" and attention shifted away from the governor.[40]

NOVEMBER 29, the day after Thanksgiving, was an official holiday in many Georgia towns. That day, the *Atlanta Journal* reported that despite chilly weather, "the city never saw a more spontaneous or heartfelt greeting from a grateful people." Roosevelt toured Fort McPherson with his son James (standing to the right of the president in the photo). The U.S. Army had established the fort in East Point, just southwest of Atlanta in 1885. (The army closed Fort McPherson in 2011.) The Roosevelts then traveled on to meet an estimated one hundred thousand students at Piedmont Park. The *Warm Springs Mirror* reported: "In an address before the most tremendous crowd in the history of the State in Atlanta last Friday, President Roosevelt covered practically all of the achievements of the New Deal. . . . Although the President made no direct declaration of his candidacy for reelection, it was the opinion of many that several of his observations were tantamount to a formal announcement."[41]

THE DAY AFTER his address at Grant Field, Roosevelt joined Marion Luther Brittain, president of Georgia Tech from 1922 to 1944, and fans to watch Georgia Tech beat Georgia 19–7 in their annual fall football classic.

UNIVERSITY HOUSING PROJECT
FOR NEGROES · ATLANTA GEORGIA
EDWARDS · SAYWARD ARCHITECTS ··· ROBERT LOGAN · ASSOCIATE
O I FREEMAN ENGINEER
PROJECT NO. 1102   1934

IN DEDICATING Techwood Homes, Roosevelt unveiled a bronze marker at the first low-cost public housing project in the United States. In his address at Grant Field, Roosevelt stated: "Your Government says to you: 'You cannot borrow your way out of debt; but you can invest your way into a sounder future.' . . . We were insolvent. Today we are solvent and we are going to stay so." As the first effort of the Housing Division of the Public Works Administration, Techwood Homes served as a pilot project for federally assisted public housing. A ten-block area along Techwood Drive, known as Tech Flats, was photographed before being cleared to make way for the housing project.

In speaking about New Deal projects to put people back to work, build roads and buildings, and more, Roosevelt stated:

> You and I are enlisted today in a great crusade in every part of the land to cooperate with Nature and not to fight her, to cooperate to stop destructive floods, to prevent dust storms, to prevent the washing away of our precious soils, to grow trees, to give thousands of farm families a chance to live, and to seek to provide more and better food for the city dwellers of the nation. . . . Aside from the tremendous increase in morale through substituting work for a dole, there is a practical side of permanent material benefit. . . . There stands a tribute to useful work under Government supervision—the first slum clearance and low-rent housing project. . . . Today those hopeless old houses are gone [from the slum clearance] and in their place we see the bright cheerful buildings of the Techwood Housing Project. . . . Recovery means something more than getting the country back into the black. You and I do not want just to go back to the past. We want to face the future in the belief that human beings can enjoy more of the good things of life, under better conditions, than human beings ever enjoyed in the past.[42]

Following his speech at Grant Field, Roosevelt greeted thousands of African American students, prompting *Time* magazine to drily note: "Then the President rolled on to Atlanta University for a Jim-Crow repetition of the same ceremony with Negro school children."[43] He also looked at University Homes, a second federal housing project. Many substandard houses were removed to make way for University Homes, and that project, which opened in 1938, had just gotten under way at the time.

ON DECEMBER 2, 1935, Roosevelt traveled fifteen miles from Warm Springs to Pine Mountain Valley in neighboring Harris County to celebrate an effort "to reestablish rural community life." Joined by Cason J. Callaway (back seat, left to right); Philip Weltner, Public Works Administration official; and Richard Morris, manager of the Pine Mountain Valley settlement, Roosevelt addressed a crowd of "hardy settlers." The group traveled in Roosevelt's open car despite the cold, blustery day. Gay Shepperson, the only female state Works Progress administrator, joined the group. As one of the first federal efforts of its kind, the valley settlement, which covered twelve thousand acres, aimed to help families suffering during the Depression and was expected to be an example for future projects.

In 1935, the community consisted of 124 four-, five-, and six-room cottages for 265 families, plus barns, a church, and a school. (A family barn is shown in this 2015 photograph.) Settlers included farm families plus textile workers who had participated in a strike against Callaway Mills earlier in the year and had been evicted from the company housing. Reluctant to join Roosevelt on this trip, Callaway told the president, "Some of our men, the ones on strike, will be there and I am not very popular right now. They might take a shot at me and hit you." At Roosevelt's insistence, Callaway went along. The day passed peaceably and ended with the president spending the night at Callaway's Blue Springs Lodge near Hamilton.[44] Bill Trotter, whose father worked for Callaway Mills, remembered hearing his father and others talk about "those socialist" projects in the countryside near Warm Springs.[45]

Roosevelt told the group of two thousand to three thousand people: "This is another case of a dream come true.

I can't tell you how happy I am about what has been accomplished here in the short space of a year. In the United States there are many, many families that need aid in reestablishing themselves, in improving their living conditions. The government has not the money to help them all, but communities of this kind point the way and illustrate to them what can and should be done."[46]

Henry Kimbrough told the group: "There used to be just a few old houses and mules hereabouts. It is hard to believe what has been done. . . . This is the greatest proposition in the United States. You will never know how much good you have done humanity."[47]

This visit signaled the start of a close relationship. During his trips to Warm Springs, Roosevelt often spent a few hours in the valley, including March 31, 1938, when children welcomed him, Mrs. Roosevelt, and Harry Hopkins with song. That November, Roosevelt visited during the community's annual harvest festival, which included a pageant featuring 550 participants and over four hundred costumes. Such welcomes included elements of paternalism, as the leader smiled down at those who lived on the land.[48] Martha Swann Wadsworth remembered dancing and singing, "Over hill, over dale, as we hit the dusty trail, Pine Mountain Valley keeps rolling along." Eleanor Roosevelt strongly supported these resettlement efforts, though she seemed more interested in Arthurdale, West Virginia. Following the president's recommendations, settlers planted grass and trees plus commercial crops and raised chickens and cows. Perhaps against his wishes, they also raised cotton as a major crop. In April 1940, Roosevelt visited and "mildly scolded other states in the U.S. for not developing cooperative resettlement programs more fully. . . . The chief executive recalled that he once had voiced hope that the states would profit by the example set in the PMV community."[49]

Ultimately, farmers in the valley struggled to make a profit, and few communities elsewhere developed. William Winn states in his description of Pine Mountain Valley that "the cooperative economy proved to be a failure. Many of the community's colonists felt themselves to be not living, breathing human beings but cogs in the wheels of a grand social design and not much different from the industrial machinery that had allegedly driven them to relief. . . . There was trouble in paradise. It began with mass meetings and proceeded to . . . forced evictions."[50] During World War II, Congress mandated the liquidation of these projects. The original investment had been about $2 million, while sales brought in about $800,000. The development included a community barn plus barns at several homesites.

ROOSEVELT FREQUENTLY VISITED this school, located in the heart of Pine Mountain Valley. Students would often sing and perform for their president. They had a special banner created. Such visits were the highlight of the year for many students. A nearby church is the only one that had Roosevelt's permission to use his name. The president wrote the church members, "I am touched by the thoughtfulness of the members in the congregation and shall feel greatly honored to have the new community Church bear my name." Residents broke ground for the church at Thanksgiving 1938, during a presidential visit. They donated their labor to build the church, while the Pine Mountain Valley Corporation furnished the land, plans, and materials. Henry Toombs designed the colonial-style church. Roosevelt himself requested that the lumber for the church be sawed from timber at his Warm Springs farm. A congregational church, nondenominational and theologically neutral in a style popular in the 1930s, the church reflected the cooperative ideals of the settlement itself.[51]

FRANKLIN ROOSEVELT and Cason Callaway shared an appreciation of the Georgia countryside, farming, and the navy. Roosevelt had been assistant secretary of the navy in World War I, while Callaway had served in the navy's Bureau of Supplies and Accounts in Washington, D.C. Evidence suggests that the two did not meet until Roosevelt started coming to Warm Springs in the 1920s, though Roosevelt wrote a letter of introduction for Cason's father, Fuller Callaway, to the U.S. Naval attaché in Paris before Callaway left on a tour of Europe as part of his duties with the World's Cotton Conference in 1919. Cason and Franklin became close friends, and the Callaways visited the White House on several occasions. During one trip to Blue Springs, the Callaway home in Hamilton, Georgia, the group had drinks at the upstairs bar, then had dinner on the main floor, where Roosevelt spent the night in a bedroom just off the living room.

Mrs. Hollis Lanier and Marvin McIntyre, Roosevelt's assistant, stand at the fireplace. By the window are Admiral Ross T. McIntire, Roosevelt's physician; Missy LeHand; Grace Tully; and Charles Rawson, Callaway's brother-in-law. Seated near the fireplace are Ben Hardaway, Mrs. Clark Howell, Mrs. Fuller E. Callaway Sr., Roosevelt, Mrs. Ben Hardaway, Mrs. Fuller E. Callaway Jr. (with the top of her head showing), James Roosevelt, and Clark Howell, publisher of the *Atlanta Constitution*. Gay Shepperson, head of Works Progress Administration efforts in Georgia, sits across the table. Months earlier, Roosevelt had ignored requests by Callaway for federal government intervention in settling textile strikes. Instead Georgia governor Eugene Talmadge sent troops to LaGrange to reestablish order in the mills.

Callaway later reflected on Roosevelt: "He had a remarkable mind. Not always thorough enough for me but with a practical knowledge in an amazing number of fields. But his greatest asset was his terrific strength. I never agreed with his program as President, but he could work harder than any man I ever saw."[52]

CHAPTER 5

Tougher Times in Georgia

ROOSEVELT did relatively little to advance the cause of African Americans during visits to Georgia, in part to avoid upsetting the status quo and fellow politicians. Eleanor Roosevelt lobbied her husband for better treatment for blacks and for a federal antilynching bill, but his main contact with blacks came through visits with farmers, cooks, valets, and musicians such as Graham Jackson. One exception to this neutral stance arose when he encouraged the building of a new school in Warm Springs.

Rev. W. G. Harry remembered that Missy LeHand called saying that the president wanted to meet with a few leading  citizens about an important matter. As mayor at the time, Harry met with Roosevelt; Sam Killian, who later became mayor; and one or two other men. Reverend Harry said that Roosevelt was emphatic about the need for a change. He remembered Roosevelt saying: "'I am just embarrassed when my friends come down here from the north and look at the Negro school building. We go up and see the white school building and then they want to know where the Negro school building is.' . . . He said 'I want something done about it and I called you fellows in here to see if you could give me any suggestions.' And a committee was appointed and efforts immediately began."[1]

Roosevelt met with trustees of the local school district and secured contributions from his friend George Foster Peabody, the Rosenwald Foundation, and private donations. The Rosenwald fund had played a significant role in education in the South in the early part of the twentieth century by building 4,977 schools in the South, 242 of them in Georgia. The program had officially ended, but Roosevelt convinced Julius Rosenwald, head of Sears Roebuck in Chicago and his family's charitable foundation, to contribute funds for one more school.

The Works Progress Administration and the Public Works Administration assisted in constructing the Eleanor Roosevelt Vocational School for Colored Youth. The cornerstone proudly proclaims the details of the name and date of construction. At the dedication ceremony on March 18, 1937, Roosevelt expressed hope that the school would inspire districts across the nation to undertake similar improvements. The male Glee Club from Fort Valley Normal and Industrial School sang spirituals, and the audience joined in a rousing rendition of "America." During his address, Roosevelt explained how he was beginning "to learn economics at Warm Springs." He realized that many in the region survived "at the mercy of people outside the South under conditions over which they had no control. . . . People were starving under five-cent cotton and the young were growing up without education. . . . We began to think of the picture as a national picture," with the aim to stabilize wages at a higher level than currently earned and increase everyone's purchasing power. He added, "Yes, we have a long way to go, but we are taking the proper steps as shown by the fact that this building . . . has been built to meet our physical needs. At the same time we must raise our economic standards a good deal higher than they are today."[2] (The school is now used for storage, and as this 2013 photo shows, its windows have been bricked over.

In accepting the building for the Educational System of Georgia, Dr. M. D. Collins described Eleanor Roosevelt as "the greatest woman—not of the year, nor of the decade, but of the century." He added that her tireless efforts to help the poor would one day mean that there would be no underprivileged children, and instead all the nation's youth would have access to the educational facilities of the nation.[3]

Eleanor, an absent honoree, was visiting Oklahoma. In her behalf Roosevelt stated: "I am also sorry that my better half cannot be here today. She asked me to tell you that she is tremendously grateful and very happy in having this fine building named in her honor, and I hope that next time we will, both of us, be able to get down here so that she may come here and see this school and see the children in it."[4]

The couple had celebrated their thirty-second wedding anniversary and Eleanor's birthday the day before by exchanging telegrams. William C. Bullitt, daughter-in-law Mrs. James C. Roosevelt, and Missy LeHand joined the president on the trip. Bullitt, who courted Missy LeHand for two years, had returned to the United States for a brief respite from his position as ambassador to France. During his week at Warm Springs, he updated the president on growing tensions between Great Britain, France, and Germany. Within two and a half years, the Second World War would have started in Europe.

ROOSEVELT MET WITH officers of the Phi Kappa Literary Society of the University of Georgia in the fall of 1937 in Warm Springs. One of the Phi Kappa members he met with was Morris B. Abram, who became an attorney and successfully challenged Georgia's county unit system of elections in 1963. He later served as president of Brandeis University.

The society wanted Roosevelt to speak or meet with its group in Athens. Roosevelt declined—he preferred to appear outdoors, at places he could quickly reach from his car, or on the ground floor of buildings. He had a couple of unpleasant experiences giving speeches on the second and third floors of buildings in the 1920s and afterward tried to avoid making speeches or dedicating buildings that required climbing steps such as would have been necessary if he appeared in the Phi Kappa building. Instead, the following year, Roosevelt spoke in the stadium at the university's summer commencement.[5] In this photograph Franklin and Eleanor are motoring near Athens in 1934. Members of the press and the general public surround the car.

ROOSEVELT VISITED GAINESVILLE on April 9, 1936, just days after much of downtown had been destroyed in one of the worst tornados ever to hit Georgia. He wrote his cousin Margaret "Daisy" Suckley about making a quick stop in Warm Springs. "I may stop in damaged areas to see if relief agencies are all functioning properly and together." He added to the letter after the visit. "We have just left Gainesville—All the relief work goes well but the tornado levelled everything over a two-mile strip two blocks wide—over 200 killed and 1,200 injured. I'm always very thankful that we have no serious tornado or flood history in Dutchess!"[6] The practice of presidents visiting disaster areas to show their concern did not become commonplace until the 1960s, when Presidents Johnson and Nixon began making such trips.[7]

Final numbers indicate that 170 people died, almost 1,000 more suffered injuries, and many buildings, including the Hall County Courthouse, lay in ruins following one of Georgia's worst natural disasters. Roosevelt visited with the heads of various relief agencies and told the crowds that he appreciated their spirit and hoped to be back soon for a happier visit.

A visit by Georgia governor Gene Talmadge a few days later left editors of the *Gainesville Eagle* less hopeful: "He said that Georgia's unselfish, even lavish, assistance made it unnecessary for federal relief. . . . The Governor is . . . wrong. . . . He made a statement as unmitigatedly malicious and pernicious as it is untrue, and he sought to further injure a town that was virtually blown off the map."[8]

Talmadge could not seek reelection since he was nearing the end of his second term. Eurith D. Rivers ran on a New Deal platform supporting most of the programs his predecessor had opposed. With Rivers as governor and renewed support for the New Deal, relief monies finally began to pour into Gainesville and Roosevelt's second state in 1937.

PRESIDENT ROOSEVELT had been scheduled to speak at the dedication of Roosevelt Square in December 1937. On December 2, the *Gainesville Eagle* proudly reported: "All the glory that was Greece and the grandeur that was Rome may well descend on Gainesville next Wednesday" when the president and first lady were expected to visit. A prophetic editorial that day proclaimed: "Perhaps outstanding in the man is his self-reliance. . . . The Chief's temper is a blue-white flame. When riled, he is bullheaded, impatient, uncompromising, and vindictive." A persistent toothache, however, forced Roosevelt to cut short his Thanksgiving holiday in Georgia and postpone the visit until spring.

On the evening of March 22, 1938, Roosevelt boarded a Southern Railway car in Washington, D.C., bound for Georgia. The train stopped the next morning in Toccoa to pick up Governor E. D. Rivers. More than four thousand people, including school children, were gathered downtown for the occasion. The president appeared on the rear of the train platform with Rivers and told the group: "We are all in the same boat, and we are all plowing the same furrow. If anything hurts you down here, it hurts the rest of the nation. If others are hurt elsewhere, it hurts you folks down here." He closed by telling them that he was coming down for ten days of rest but added, "I hope to find time to talk over matters of national and state importance with the people of the state," giving a forewarning of the hard-hitting speech he would deliver later that day in Gainesville as citizens dedicated Roosevelt Square.[9] Later that day, as the president continued his journey, the train slowed near Alto and blew the whistle for patients as it passed the Georgia State Tubercular Sanitarium.

In Gainesville, between twenty-five thousand and sixty thousand people gathered to hear the president dedicate a three-block civic center, which included the Federal Building and post office, the courthouse, and City Hall, plus a monument honoring Roosevelt. At the time, this was the only known memorial to him in America. On an overcast day, the Georgia Tech band played an impromptu "It Ain't Gonna Rain No More" just before the president arrived. The rains held until after his departure. Roosevelt greeted the crowds by telling them: "Although I have lived for a time in Middle Georgia, I take pride in the fact that the blood of North

Georgia runs in the veins of my children," a reference to Martha "Mittie" Bulloch Roosevelt, grandmother of his wife, Eleanor. After being introduced by Senator Walter F. George, Roosevelt addressed the crowd: "Gainesville suffered a great disaster. So did the nation in those eight years of false prosperity followed by four years of collapse. Gainesville showed a united front for the good of its whole population, rich and poor alike. It rose to rebuild on sounder lines. Today the U.S. is rising and rebuilding on sounder lines. We propose to go forward and not back."[10]

His speech then took a sharper tone as he classified the South as a low-wage area. He surprised many by calling on industries to increase wages and asserted that progress was being retarded by "selfishness on the part of a few," adding, "If Gainesville had been faced with that type of minority selfishness your city would not stand rebuilt as it is today." He declared that Georgians and Southerners "must face the facts. . . . Most men and women who work for wages in this whole area get wages which are far too low. On the present scale of wages . . . the South cannot and will not succeed in establishing successful new industries, as we ought to." Roosevelt announced that prosperity was being slowed by a "selfish minority . . . who give little thought to the 'one-third ill fed, ill clad, and ill-housed' and who regard balancing the budget as far more important than appropriating for relief." He added a stinging punch: "When you come down to it, there is little difference between the feudal system and the Fascist system."[11]

On April 4, 1938, editors of the *Gainesville Eagle* stated: "The Eagle does not believe Roosevelt had Gainesville, or similar cities with similar industries, in mind when the accusation was made," though they resented Roosevelt for mentioning the issues of low wages and feudalism in their town.

The incident received national press coverage. *Time* magazine compared the uproar caused by Roosevelt to that created when Secretary of Labor Frances Perkins commented on shoelessness in Dixie. Editors further insulted Georgians by commenting on the "tobacco-chewing crowd" that had been insulted by the president.[12]

EDITORS OF LOCAL NEWSPAPERS chafed against Roosevelt's comments criticizing the South's economy. The people of North Georgia had gathered to honor their president and instead had been slandered. His comments were considered unjustified, and the fact that a few people in a huge crowd might have been chewing tobacco did not warrant insulting the entire group. Local citizens thought the president had insulted their area by comparing it to a feudal state, but the national magazine insulted their dignity!

With this speech, Roosevelt's relationship with the South began to change. Historian Frank Freidel observes, "Despite all the years Roosevelt had been visiting Warm Springs, and demonstrating his mastery of Southern social and political mores in the guise of a Georgia farmer-politician, he stood revealed now as an outsider, at best a meddler, and at worst a Yankee carpetbagger."[13]

Two days after the Gainesville address, Henry H. Revill, editor of the *Meriwether Vindicator*, acknowledged the controversy: "We welcome you with our heart love and bid you enjoy the rest you so richly deserve. You are secure from all alarms in Meriwether; no carping criticism to greet you; no danger can befall you. The locked shields of your friends and neighbors surround you."[14]

EN ROUTE from Gainesville to Warm Springs, the president's train stopped in Griffin for a brief afternoon visit. He greeted a crowd of ten thousand or so who braved a downpour to see their president and neighbor. Griffin and Spalding County schools closed early that afternoon, enabling schoolchildren to attend. The train pulled into the Griffin Depot (shown in the photo), and Marvin McIntyre appeared on the rear platform followed by Congressman E. M. Owen of Griffin. Secret Service and National Guardsmen kept an eye on the large crowd. Then the president appeared and accepted flowers from young Henrietta Carlisle, daughter of the secretary of the chamber of commerce, who presented him "Griffin Grown Flowers." Roosevelt assured the crowd that he was happy to be in Georgia, especially since spring would arrive soon.[15] He shared a story he had told Callaway Mills overseers years earlier about a local saloon in Warm Springs known as Griffin, where men spent the day while their wives thought they were in Spalding County on business. The site of the saloon had since become part of the quadrangle at the Warm Springs Foundation, and Roosevelt assured them, "It is serving a much better use than it did in the old days."[16]

A WEEK LATER, as many as fifty thousand people greeted Roosevelt when he stopped in Columbus on his way to Fort Benning on March 30. People gathered at the Muscogee County Courthouse or stood along a seven-mile route. Accompanied by Eleanor, the president told the audience: "I am glad to come back after a few years, glad to see the fine progress that has been made in this city, in this county, in this part of Georgia because I think back fifteen to twenty years, it looks to me as after all on every hand we can see the improvement in the process of living in the State of Georgia."[17]

Roosevelt and city leaders gathered under a large shade tree. The *Columbus Ledger-Enquirer* proclaimed: "It was history in the making, the movement of national affairs across the local stage—the stage of our lives."[18]

In 1934, citizens of Columbus donated the Columbus Colonnade to the foundation. In accepting the gift, Roosevelt had commented: "We all know that if it had not been for the good people of Columbus, Georgia, there would not have been any Warm Springs. . . . I shall always be grateful to them for their helpfulness at that time and later on during the difficult transition. I shall always be grateful to them for the great help that they have given in so many ways since then."[19]

THE COMMANDER IN CHIEF made several appearances at military bases in Georgia, including this trip to Fort Benning in March 1938, to review army troops. Joining Franklin and Eleanor in this photo is Georgia governor E. D. Rivers in the car. Also in the group saluting the U.S. flag are Columbus mayor L. C. Wilson; Brig. Gen. Asa L. Singleton, commander of Fort Benning; and Lt. Col. L. P. Hunt. Soldiers gave Roosevelt a twenty-one-gun salute, and he spent forty-five minutes touring the base and infantry school and seeing military exercises.

THE ROOSEVELTS stopped in Chipley (now Pine Mountain) during a visit to Georgia in November 1939. Children lined the streets and waved to their president as they did any time they knew he would be passing through town. Left to right in this photograph are Tap Bennett, superintendent of Pine Mountain Valley Resettlement; Jim Gillis; the Roosevelts; Mr. Starling; Henry Kimbrough; W. L. Miller, chairman of the Georgia Highway Commission; and Clem Wright. Behind Eleanor is William Hassett, the president's assistant. They stopped to discuss highway improvements with Harris County citizens. Earlier in the day, the Roosevelts met with the press at Warm Springs and discussed the idea of creating a special tax to increase national defense funds by $500 million.

Several years earlier, Roosevelt had traveled to Chipley to buy a mule. He went to "Uncle Henry" Kimbrough's trading barn and picked out his animal. Thinking he might get good publicity out of the trade, Kimbrough offered a good price, which was accepted. A few weeks later, word got back to Georgia that Roosevelt had told New Yorkers he was doing all right as a farmer in Georgia because he made forty dollars in his first deal with Henry Kimbrough. A few months later, Roosevelt sent word that he needed another mule for farming. Kimbrough brought a mule, got a check from Roosevelt, and then declared that he had gotten his forty dollars back! Roosevelt is reported to have roared with laughter.[20]

AFTER A ROUND of public addresses and visits, Roosevelt boarded a train to return to Washington on April 3, 1938, joined by advisor Harry Hopkins (shown in the photo) and Eleanor Roosevelt. Eleanor had arrived in Warm Springs a week after her husband. Their son James Roosevelt stated that they had once discussed Franklin's reentry into politics following his bout with polio. She assured him that she supported her husband. "I thought it would be good for him. I thought it would help him break away from Warm Springs before he became too deeply entrenched in running that resort."[21]

GREETED BY AREA RESIDENTS since his first visit to Warm Springs in October 1924, Roosevelt met larger and larger crowds as his political stature grew. Through the years, his arrivals and departures became major social events. Robert Copeland remembered putting work aside on such occasions. "When we found out that Roosevelt was coming down on the train . . . my daddy let us leave the farm to come down and see him disboard the train at Warm Springs. When he came down off the train, he would raise his hat, 'Hello Warm Springs, Hello Warm Springs.' We would stay there till he left for the Foundation and then we'd go back to the farm."[22] The need for greater security during World War II ended advance knowledge of his travel plans, though the sudden presence of a large number of military guards always signaled his imminent arrival.

This group gathered in August 1938, during a rare summertime visit. The president made a brief stop at the Little White House, had lunch with Georgia governor E. D. Rivers and Lawrence Camp, a U.S. district attorney who was seeking the Democratic nomination to the U.S. Senate, and then boarded the train for a controversial trip to Athens and Barnesville. Basil O'Connor joined him on the train. The local press anticipated trouble. The *Warm Springs Mirror* reported on August 5: "Political leaders have speculated upon the possibility that Mr. Roosevelt will make some reference in his address to the Georgia campaign" between Walter F. George, Eugene Talmadge, and Camp.

FRANKLIN D. ROOSEVELT participated in graduation ceremonies at several Georgia colleges and universities. He gave the commencement address at the Fourth District A&M school in Carrollton in 1929 and received an honorary degree from Oglethorpe University in 1932. The University of Georgia awarded him an honorary doctorate of laws degree on August 11, 1938. Captured with him in the photograph, Georgia chancellor S. V. Sanford, in full academic regalia, presented the degree as aide Col. Edwin Watson and Governor E. D. Rivers watched. Roosevelt was the third president to visit Athens—James Monroe had visited in 1819, president-elect William Howard Taft in 1908. Herbert Hoover made a speech at the campus before being elected to the office of president.

Twenty-two thousand people packed the north stands of the stadium at Athens. Hundreds more stood on the grass-covered banks, while many lined the streets between the railroad station and the stadium to throw confetti. Home owners decorated their houses, leading the *Athens Banner-Herald* to declare the group to be "one of the most colorful crowds in the history of the City."[23]

One university student, Frank Wells, quipped, "I graduated with the President" after receiving his BA in journalism. In the *Athens Banner-Herald*, Wells declared: "The President's speech was effective because of its shortness. It was indeed a grand speech to deliver at a graduation."[24]

With typewriters in tow, the press had field-level seats. Roosevelt talked about economic and educational conditions and mentioned how the constitution of Georgia mandated public schools. He lamented:

> School after school in the rural districts of the State—and most of the districts are rural districts—was open only four or five months a year. . . . Apparently a law or a clause in the Constitution was not enough. . . . It was due to lack of money. . . . The taxable values were not there. . . . The actual going values of property were so meagre that, when taxes on those values were collected, the sum received could not pay for adequate teachers or proper equipment. Public education was therefore dependent on public wealth. Public wealth was too low to support good schools. . . . Therefore . . . the best way for your National Government to assist state and local educational objectives is to tackle the national aspects of economic problems—to eliminate discriminations between one part of the country and another—to raise purchasing power . . . to save the waste and the erosion of our natural resources, to encourage each section to become finally independent, to take the lead in establishing social security.[25]

Roosevelt met with Moina Michael, internationally known as the "Poppy Lady," before he left Athens. Famous for her humanitarian work, she presented him with a basket of orchid dahlias. The president motored back to the train station and left Athens at 11:30 a.m. The *Banner-Herald* reported that the train "took with it one of the most beloved persons that the country has ever had. . . . One of the greatest days that the City has ever known came to a close with the departure, never to be forgotten—to be remembered for years and years to come."[26]

ROOSEVELT'S was the first honorary degree presented by the university since the establishment of the Board of Regents in 1932. Regent George Foster Peabody, who first introduced Roosevelt to Warm Springs, suggested the degree before his death in March 1938. University officials saw it as a way to strengthen ties between the university and the president. An enthusiastic crowd gathered at the site, where a long ramp had been constructed for Roosevelt to go from the car to the platform. Several decades passed before the school awarded another honorary degree. Events later in the day at Barnesville, where Roosevelt attacked Georgia senator Walter George, darkened memories for many. As Stephen Gurr notes in his biography of S. V. Sanford, "Most Georgians seemed to separate their devotion to Roosevelt from what they considered his misplaced sentiments about Senator George. Barnesville did not ruin Georgia for Roosevelt; it simply took a lot of the shine off the events of the morning in Athens and clouded the chancellor's day."[27]

ROOSEVELT ATTENDED the dedication of the Rural
Electrification Administration in Barnesville partially at the
suggestion of longtime advisors Harlee Branch, later president
of Georgia Power, and Harvey Kennedy, a Barnesville attorney.
They knew that farmers who supported REA would comprise a
majority of the audience. In addressing the crowd gathered in
Memorial Stadium at Gordon Military Institute on August 11,
1938, Roosevelt proclaimed the REA one of the most successful
innovations of the New Deal.

Roosevelt gave the audience a glimpse into how the REA had
come into existence. After buying property at Warm Springs, he
realized that he was paying exorbitant prices for electricity—operating electric lights at Warm Springs cost four times as much as at
Hyde Park. This realization led Roosevelt to study utility charges
around the country. He stated: "It can be said that a little cottage in Warm Springs, Georgia, was the birthplace of the REA."
(Despite being credited as the birthplace of the REA, the Little
White House was and remains a Georgia Power customer.)

Roosevelt also gained an awareness of the need for electricity
in rural areas as he drove around the countryside. One day in the
mid-1920s, after speaking in LaGrange, Roosevelt stopped at a
store in Mountville, between LaGrange and Greenville. He saw
that blocks of ice cooled soft drinks and people used hand pumps
to add air to tires. He and store owner Owen Caudle discussed
the need for electric lines outside cities. Such fact-finding conversations led Roosevelt to believe that social advancement would
follow the electric lines. He assured the audience at Barnesville
that electricity was "a modern necessity of life and *not a luxury*."[28]
In its two years of existence, the rural electrification program was
already making great strides in electrifying Georgia and the nation
and had put hundreds of men to work stringing power lines and
installing poles.

ROOSEVELT CHOSE the dedication of the REA in Barnesville to launch a major attack against conservative southern politicians, particularly Georgia senator Walter F. George. The mayor of Barnesville had invited George to the event. Polls indicated that two-thirds of the American people (and even more in the South) solidly supported Roosevelt and the New Deal. In his annoyance at the U.S. Senate for not supporting his efforts to add new and friendlier members to the Supreme Court, Roosevelt decided to attack George and others because they "did not speak the same language." Standing on the podium at Barnesville in this photograph are, left to right, Georgia governor E. D. Rivers; Roosevelt holding the arm of aide Col. Edwin "Pa" Watson; Virginia Polhill Price of Louisville, Georgia; a member of the National Democratic Executive Committee; and Senator Richard B. Russell Jr., the master of ceremonies. Senator George was also on the podium, while John M. Carmody, REA administrator, waited in the audience.

Decades later, residents who at the time were mostly youngsters had vivid memories of that day. They remembered that more people visited than had ever been in town, and they could still almost feel the intense heat of that afternoon. They laughed over the fact that the town ran out of Coca-Colas, which sold for five cents a bottle. They remembered being instructed not to photograph Roosevelt as he walked. They also recalled the frustrations of dealing with bureaucrats and security: the Ladies Club chose a five-year-old girl, wearing a new dress, to present a bouquet of flowers to the president, but the Secret Service vetoed the presentation.

More than a hundred laborers of the Works Progress Administration had spent two years transforming a swamp and gully into an outdoor stadium. In introducing the

president, Richard B. Russell, an alumnus of Gordon Military Institute, declared:

> As we stand here today, we see all about us the conclusive evidence of the permanent values we have received from the national program of useful building and recovery which replaced the era of do-nothing and disintegration. Where we now stand and enjoy this magnificent stadium was once a swamp. As a schoolboy, I well remember how we always felt that a trip down through the ravine and across the tanyard branch was a visit to the wilderness. . . . Every section of this nation, and every segment of American life has benefited in this building of a greater and better United States.[29]

He noted: "There has been reserved to us here in Georgia, near his second home, the honor and privilege of having the President of the United States on Georgia soil to participate for the first time in the dedication of a Rural Electrification project. . . . We recognize in him not only the preserver of our American institutions, but the greatest exponent of liberal democracy and equality of opportunity in the history of this republic."[30]

At the end of his talk, Roosevelt forgot to press the button to release current or announce: "Let there be light." H. L. Smith, president of the Lamar Light Electric Membership Corporation, turned on the electricity despite the lack of assistance from the leader of the land.

In June and July, tensions about the coming congressional elections had begun heating up. Walter George and Roosevelt exchanged letters, concluding that while they might disagree about political and economic issues, they could remain friends. Fearing controversy, officials of the Lamar Electric Membership Corporation pledged before the event: "Realizing that President Franklin D. Roosevelt, part-time citizen of Georgia, is paying our REA project, our county, and our city a distinct honor in visiting our community on August 11th to dedicate our project . . . we the undersigned . . . therefore urge our people to lay aside all political differences. . . . We therefore urge all candidates . . . to refrain from campaigning in Lamar County and to refrain from the use of partisan banners and posters until after the President's visit on August 11, 1938."[31]

An article that appeared in the *Atlanta Constitution* about the perceived effort to limit the president's remarks prompted Lamar EMC president Smith to telegram Roosevelt: "The people of Lamar County feel that you have a right to speak on any subject you want to. . . . The facts are that we are overjoyed at your coming. . . . Please come early and stay late and say whatever you care to while you are our guest."[32]

THE PRESIDENT HIMSELF ignored the pledge to refrain from politics as the dedication turned into a rally. In his speech, Roosevelt sharply criticized George's conservative voting patterns. He told the crowd: "You, the people of Georgia, in the coming Senatorial primary, for example, have a perfect right to choose any candidate you wish. I do not seek to impair that right. . . . but because Georgia has been good enough to call me her adopted son . . . I feel no hesitation in telling you what I would do if I could vote here next month. . . . my old friend the senior Senator [George] . . . cannot possibly in my judgment be classified as belonging to the liberal school of thought."[33]

Residents remember that the audience of twenty thousand to thirty thousand people received Roosevelt's speech coolly, with boos sprinkled through the crowd. *Time* added that Roosevelt excommunicated George "as completely as any Pope ever cut off from grace an unrepentant sinner."[34] Afterward, the president and George shook hands, and the senator told the president that he accepted the challenge to fight for his good name and his democratic beliefs.

The editor of the *Barnesville News Gazette* reported on August 18 that the open endorsement of Lawrence Camp for the U.S. Senate by the president of the United States had provoked many comments. On August 25, the editor referred to "the Barnesville incident" by stating: "What more could be expected from the President, for he must have his way regardless of everything and everybody."[35]

The public attack breathed new energy and vigor into George's campaign. He won reelection to the U.S. Senate, receiving 141,000 votes versus 103,000 for Eugene Talmadge and 77,000 for Lawrence Camp (shown in the photo with Roosevelt). Voters in Warm Springs supported their adopted

son, but not with their usual overwhelming numbers. They cast 150 votes for Camp, 65 for George, and 42 for Talmadge. Barnesville and George's reelection marked the worst defeat that Roosevelt suffered in Georgia. E. D. Rivers, a strong New Deal supporter, was reelected governor, indicating that New Deal sentiment in Georgia remained alive and strong. The defeat of Camp reflected resentment toward the president for interfering. As one South Georgia farmer stated, "We Georgians are Georgians as hell."[36] In resisting efforts to purge the Senate of opponents, Georgians voted much as people in South Carolina, Maryland, and elsewhere did. They resented the president's "meddling" in state elections. These feelings had faded somewhat by the time of the next presidential election, in 1940. The citizens of Lamar County apparently forgot their anger. Roosevelt lost only 2 percent of the votes between 1936 and 1940 going from 92.4 percent in 1936, when he received 839 out of 908 votes cast, to 90.6 percent in 1940, with 869 votes out of a total of 959.

Time magazine concluded an article on Barnesville with a paragraph on the mayor's driving. Mayor J. A. Cason, one of the organizers and a strong supporter of George, drove his car "like a wild man, scaring his passengers," including Basil O'Connor and an assistant to the attorney general, Joseph Keenan. The men almost got into a fistfight. The mayor's wife refused to drive Roosevelt's secretaries Marvin McIntyre and Steve Early. (Harvey Kennedy had written McIntyre on July 28: "I have discussed with you the antagonistic attitude of the Mayor and you suggested having someone else ride with the President.") Years later, local residents remembered the mayor's furor and the discontent of those present.[37]

Local newspapers questioned the leadership of their president. In March and again in August, Roosevelt had criticized Georgians. The editor of the *Meriwether Vindicator*, a vocal supporter of Roosevelt, stated: "No man agrees with everything he has done. He has made mistakes, but who hasn't. It is human to err."[38]

Herman Talmadge, son of Governor Eugene Talmadge and a dominant figure in Georgia politics from 1948 to 1981, when he served as governor and U.S. senator, summed up the attack. "The minute Roosevelt attacked Senator George, he ceased to be the great white father in Washington and became another Yankee carpetbagger. . . . What Roosevelt succeeded in doing was turning Walter George into some kind of martyr. Here Papa [Eugene Talmadge] had been trying to portray George as a Washington insider who had lost touch with the people, and the No. 1 insider had just gone denouncing him."[39] Roosevelt boosted George in that Senate election and destroyed Eugene Talmadge's strongest bid to represent his state in the Senate.

A careful and calculating politician, Roosevelt thought that as a fellow taxpayer and friend, he had a right to make such suggestions, but citizens of the state disagreed. Eleanor Roosevelt commented, "From Franklin I learned that a good politician is marked to a great extent by his sense of timing. He says the right thing at the right moment. . . . I do not mean that Franklin never made mistakes; most of the time, however, his judgment was good."[40] In this case, Roosevelt misjudged Georgians by getting involved in state elections. He went from being a beloved neighbor to being part of a meddling federal government.

ILL FEELINGS between Roosevelt and Georgia's political leaders remained long after the fall elections. Richard Russell refused to support Camp, who had once been his campaign manager. He sent George a telegram after his victory: "Heartiest congratulations on your victory," to which George responded, "Grateful for your message and interest. We had a great victory."[41]

On January 20, 1939, after rumors and problems in dealing with patronage in federal jobs in Georgia, Russell wrote Harvey Kennedy:

I have been loyal to the President even though I have not agreed with him on every detail, and I certainly do not propose to commit myself in advance to agree to anything which may be proposed, particularly when I see how Georgia and the South have

been discriminated against in the distribution of the benefits that I and some other Southern Senators have helped to create. Of course, it is tremendously unpleasant to be forced into a position of antagonism to one's own crowd, particularly when you have tried to help fight some of their battles, if not all."[42]

Conflicts between Georgia relief officials and the federal government, which had started during the Talmadge administration, continued. On November 23, 1938, Governor E. D. Rivers announced: "The President is correct in his statement that the national administration has been very indulgent and considerate in helping Georgia participate in the PWA." Roosevelt had complained that Georgia was not cooperating with the public works program and "would not get another red cent until it did."[43] Three days later, Roosevelt wrote James Farley: "Down here in Georgia, there is a rather definite tendency to quit fighting the Administration and to try to 'make-up.' . . . This tendency does not apply to some . . . like . . . Walter George. I think Dick Russell will be more inclined to go along."[44]

John Egerton, in *Speak Now against the Day: The Generation before the Civil Rights Movement in the South*, argues that election losses in 1938 signaled the unofficial end of the New Deal as the focus of the nation began to shift from the national to the international arena.[45] That November, Roosevelt arrived back at the Warm Springs Depot just as he had for most of the fourteen previous Novembers. Hugh R. Wilson, American envoy to Germany; William Phillips, ambassador to Italy; and Marvin McIntyre, one of his secretaries,

joined the president. The group is shown here in a car beside the Warm Springs depot. The United Press reported: "Mr. Roosevelt had explored the broad phases of anti-Semitism in both countries with the ambassadors as well as the plight of Catholics and Protestants in Germany."[46] Local newspapers began reporting about the dangers in Europe due to threats from Communists, Nazis, and Fascists. The *Meriwether Vindicator* declared: "President Roosevelt is devoting all his efforts to keeping his country out of war, and at the same time endeavoring to prepare this country for any eventuality that may come."[47] At this point, Roosevelt and others thought that mass resettlement of German Jews was the only solution to the problems being faced by European Jews, but places for Jews to colonize were needed. During his stay at Warm Springs, the president met with Senate and House Democratic leaders about programs for the new Congress convening in January 1939, announced several judicial appointments, and discussed continuing efforts to combat polio with national and Warm Springs leaders.[48]

After the United States declared war in 1941, Secret Service agent Mike Reilly and presidential secretary Steve Early concluded that Roosevelt should have more protection when he traveled. The Pullman Company decided that the *Ferdinand Magellan* should be armor plated; a few other improvements were made at the same time, such as enlarging the dining room and the observation car. Soon electric elevators replaced the steps on either side of the car, eliminating the need for the ramp and the arduous walk off the train.[49]

ON MARCH 30, 1939, President Roosevelt visited Alabama, where he inspected Tuskegee Institute and Alabama Polytechnic Institute at Auburn before motoring to West Point, LaGrange, Chipley, and Warm Springs for two weeks' rest.

One photograph taken that day captured West Point businessman J. Smith Lanier and the waving president riding past a background of people and buildings. Lanier had met with Roosevelt a few years earlier when he sought support for an east-west highway from Savannah to Macon to Warm Springs to West Point. In another photo, the president rides through downtown LaGrange, where an estimated four thousand people lined Broad Street and North Court Square to greet him. The square stood vacant at the time because the courthouse had burned in 1936 and a fountain and a statue of the Marquis de LaFayette were years away from reality. Roosevelt declined an invitation from LaGrange mayor R. S. O'Neal to address the crowd. Here, as elsewhere, police had trouble keeping the roads clear of people wanting a closer glimpse of their president.

SEVERAL ADVISORS came to Warm Springs numerous times, including Harry Hopkins, shown in this photo at an informal press conference. Hopkins described his trip to Warm Springs between March 30 and April 9, 1939.

We left Washington early in the afternoon. . . . There is no one here but Missy—the President and me . . . ever so informal and altogether pleasant. And why not. I like Missy—the President is the grandest of companions—I rest for hours—and sleep ever so well. The food around the W. H. menage is medium to downright bad.

The President wakes up about eight thirty—breakfast in bed—reads the morning papers and if left alone will spend a half hour or so reading a detective story. I would go in about nine-thirty—usually much talk of European affairs—Kennedy and Bullitt our ambassadors in London and Paris would telephone—Hull and Welles from State Department so we had the latest news of Hitler's moves in the international checkerboard. His secretaries and aides would come in about ten thirty with mail, schedule of appointments—gossip of the foundation—light chit-chat for half an hour when the President dressed before going to the pool for his daily treatment at eleven. He may keep an appointment before eleven—gets in his little car—drives by the press cottage for an interview—this takes about twenty minutes—after the pool he will drive by the golf links—home for lunch at one.

Lunch has usually been F.D.R. with Missy and me—these are the pleasantest because he is under no restraint and personal and public business is discussed with the utmost frankness. . . . He will sleep a bit after lunch—and at three drive over the country-side with a guest—visit his farm—look at the new tree plantings—back around four-thirty for an hour's dictation. Then relax till dinner at seven. The ceremonial cocktail with the President doing the honors—gin and grapefruit juice is his current favorite. . . . Dinner therefore is gay—as it should be—and the President reminisces long over the personal experiences of his life—he tells incidents well—tho he has a bad habit of repeating them every year or so. I fancy Missy has heard them all many times but she never flickers an eyebrow.

After dinner the President retreats to his stamps—magazines and an evening paper. George Fox comes in to give him a rub down and the President is in bed by ten.[50]

GEORGIA CONGRESSMAN CARL VINSON

(center) and others joined Roosevelt in his car during the summer of 1938. In November, the entire Georgia congressional delegation scheduled a meeting with the president for the first time. Others in the party included Richard B. Russell Jr., Eugene Cox, Malcolm Tarver, Robert Ramspect, Stephen Pace, Ben Gibbs, and Sidney Camp. Invited by Vinson but not by the president, Senator Walter George did not attend. The visit was informal and the "conversations barren of politics."[53]

Vinson chaired the U.S. House Naval Affairs Committee from 1931 until 1947. Roosevelt loved the navy and had been an assistant secretary, but he and Vinson disagreed about how strong the navy should be, how many ships it should have, and the appropriate ratio of officers to enlisted men. Despite threatening developments in Europe, Roosevelt hesitated to give the appearance that the United States had begun preparing for war.

As the reality of war became stronger, Roosevelt's trips to Warm Springs came less frequently. In 1941, the president visited once with intentions of staying for two weeks. Rev. W. G. Harry recalled that Roosevelt attended church services in November 1941. During this trip, local townspeople and patients and staff at the institute heard Roosevelt voice his fear that war would come before his next visit.[54]

At Thanksgiving dinner, he expressed his hope that Warm Springs would continue to grow and make progress. On a reflective note, he told the audience:

> We need to be thoroughly thankful that these years of peace were given to us. At the same time, we should think not only of our own selfish purposes for this country of ours, but also think a little bit about other people, people in countries which have been overrun, people in countries which have been attacked, and, yes, people in those countries which are doing the attacking. . . . It may be that next Thanksgiving these boys of the Military Academy and of the Naval Academy will be actually fighting for the defense of these American institutions of ours.[55]

Yielding to his concerns about the international situation, he cut his visit short and returned to Washington, D.C. A week later, he asked Congress to declare war on Japan after the bombing of Pearl Harbor. Roosevelt failed to visit Warm Springs at all in 1942 and spent only two days there in 1943. During these stressful days of wartime, he had little time to rest as his health began to fail.

ROOSEVELT has stopped his car in front of Georgia Hall at the Warm Springs Foundation. Walking around the car are Canadian prime minister W. L. Mackenzie King, followed by assistants William D. Hassett, Thomas Qualters, and others. The group visited Warm Springs between April 19 and 27, 1940. An authorized statement declared this a social visit between old friends, though newsmen were skeptical since Canada was at war.[51] At the beginning of the week, the press had reported that Roosevelt's train would be ever ready to take the president back to Washington should conditions worsen in Europe.[52] During the weeklong visit, Roosevelt delivered a national radio broadcast announcing that he planned to take a three-week trip around the country early in the summer.

ROOSEVELT often stopped to talk to reporters gathered for a roadside press conference. One apparently took place in the parking lot of Georgia Hall. He usually held at least two conferences a week with members of the press in Warm Springs. Topics discussed varied widely, including local activities in Warm Springs, the latest actions of Adolf Hitler, the affairs of the District of Columbia, and the housing needs of the nation. Roosevelt genuinely seemed to enjoy meeting with the press in Warm Springs. He sometimes kidded with reporters, and he openly cultivated their support for his policies and for Warm Springs. They respected his privacy and helped hide his disability.[56]

Roosevelt often used his Warm Springs meetings with the press to float "trial balloons" to see how the media would deal with a topic or a troublesome issue and try to shape public opinion. Such press activity could be more easily accomplished in the informal confines at Warm Springs or even Hyde Park than in Washington, D.C. During his visit in the fall of 1935, *Time* reported that Roosevelt passed the word about extensive federal budget cuts that he wanted as a New Year's present for the county. He made such comments about budget cuts to warn people that the budget might include surprises and to reduce the shock of the actual cuts.[57] During a 1939 visit, he mentioned that the country needed to move toward greater war readiness and that "some consideration was being given the idea of a special tax to finance expenditures for national defense."[58]

The gatherings seemed informal, sometimes with casually dressed reporters, but Roosevelt met only designated members of the press corps and rarely with independent newsmen while at Warm Springs. Designated members of the press had to pay to stay at Warm Springs. In December 1935, a company had to pay $7.00 a day to keep a reporter in town. Twelve newsmen stayed in a five-room cottage "with two Negro boys to feed and care for them." Rooms could be had by the general public for $5.00 a night in the nearby Tuscawilla Hotel, though rates in comparable hotels when the president was not visiting cost only about $1.50 or $2.00 a night.[59]

Political leaders also enjoyed the slower pace at the Little White House. U.S. Secretary of the Interior Harold Ickes remembered playing poker during a December 1934 visit. "Until I played on this occasion . . . I don't think that I have played poker for twenty-five or thirty years. However, at Warm Springs it furnished occasion for some social times. None of us lost enough money to hurt and it was good fun."[60]

CHAPTER 6

Commander in Chief

AS EARLY AS SPRING of 1939, Roosevelt waved good-bye at the Warm Springs Depot, cautioning those gathered: "I'll be back in the fall if we don't have a war." Later that year, Roosevelt told those gathered for Thanksgiving dinner: "I am in favor of war. I am very much in favor of war, the kind of war that we are conducting here at Warm Springs, the kind of war that, aided and abetted by what we have been doing at Warm Springs now for fourteen or fifteen years, is spreading all over the country—the war against the crippling of men and women and, especially of children." He then assured the group that even if war came, he hoped to come down at least for a few days "to see how the Warm Springs family [was] getting on."[1]

During his brief 1941 visit, he joined polio patients for a belated Thanksgiving dinner and stories about past dinners. He also saw Missy LeHand, who was at Warm Springs recovering from two strokes she had suffered earlier in the year. He soon rushed back to Washington to deal with threats from the Japanese. He later said he had arrived that morning with "one of those psychological things, a hunch."[2] Then on December 7, he asked Congress to declare war against Japan following the bombing of Pearl Harbor.

In 1942, he did not visit but, in March, deeded his twenty-six-hundred-acre farm (not including the Little White House) to the Warm Springs Foundation along with equipment and stock. In 1943, twenty-four hours in mid-April had to suffice for a visit. Roosevelt traveled through Georgia to inspect military bases, including Fort Benning and Fort Oglethorpe. In this photograph, he finds a little time to play with Fala in the White House study in 1943. Since Fala's birth in 1940, he had been a popular visitor whenever he got to travel with the president and became one of the most popular presidential pets ever.

ON APRIL 17, 1943, Roosevelt paid an unadvertised visit to the Third Women's Army Auxiliary Training Corp at Fort Oglethorpe in Chickamauga National Park in northwest Georgia. He saw nearly three thousand young women parade by for formal review during his first visit to a Women's Army Auxiliary Corps WAAC training center. He also visited Fort Benning. The *Warm Springs Mirror* reported on April 23, 1943, that "he sat in on several open-air classes for officer candidates. At one class he sat less than 100 feet from the line of fire of machine guns and mortars spitting out live and tracer ammunition into an 'enemy' position." Roosevelt's southern stops included Camp Forrest, Tennessee; Parris Island, South Carolina; and Maxwell Field, Alabama, as he made his second major trip to observe expanding war efforts around the nation. He then traveled on to Mexico to meet its president.

AT FORT OGLETHORPE, he met with Col. Oveta Culp Hobby (shown in the photo). An attorney and a journalist, she became director of the Women's Army Auxiliary Corps and was the first female commanding officer in the U.S. Army. She later served as secretary of the newly created Department of Health, Education, and Welfare (HEW) under President Dwight D. Eisenhower.

Roosevelt's distant cousin Margaret "Daisy" Suckley traveled with him in 1943. They also visited Fort Benning. Suckley wrote in her diary that they witnessed a "problem, a battle in which they use real ammunition. . . . It was beautifully put on and one can see its great value in training. . . . It

was a beautiful day, but, for this season, very chilly, the wind blew, and we travelled through the area in a cloud of dust. F. [Franklin] in an open car . . . forty miles to Warm Springs."[3]

At Georgia Hall, they had a turkey dinner, perhaps making up for the missed Thanksgiving meal the previous year. Suckley recorded: "There were 100 patients in all . . . the great majority in wheel chairs. . . . F. . . . made a serious, soft-voiced little speech . . . then was wheeled to the door of the dining room where he stayed to shake hands with each patient that filed through. . . . It was an experience for them all . . . a perfect day for F.D.R. at Warm Springs. He was very happy, surrounded by old friends who love him."[4]

Roosevelt told the group, "I don't have to tell the Warm Springs family how very happy I am to be back with *us* again. I have really stolen these few moments—just twenty-four hours. I am not here. You may read about it in another week." Roosevelt was alluding to the fact that this was one of his few trips to Warm Springs when the press did not know he was coming and did not have a full agenda of his planned events. He urged them to be prepared for an influx of men and women in uniform since infantile paralysis did not respect age or position in society and cautioned, "We must always remember that we still have a duty to the civilian population of the country."[5] The following day, Roosevelt went for a swim in the pools and spent time with friends. Suckley concluded: "F. was visibly expanding and blossoming all day . . . to the Knob for a picnic lunch . . . fish chowder, sandwiches, deviled eggs. . . . The country is very dry, the roads dusty. Mrs. [C. E.] Irwin (wife of the chief surgeon) remarked that they once suggested surfacing the roads to avoid dust. The P. [President] answered that 'we want to keep things simple.' So no more is said about it. The place IS F.D.R."[6]

DESPITE HAVING LITTLE TIME to visit Warm Springs, Roosevelt stayed involved in activities at the Little White House through contacts and correspondence. Late in 1943, Fred Botts wrote Grace Tully, Roosevelt's private secretary, about a pine behind the house that needed to be cut. A guard feared that the tree might be blown onto the deck of the house during a storm due to a rock pressing into the trunk and its position on the edge of the ravine. Miss Tully replied: "I have shown it [your letter] to the President and he asks me to thank you and to say that if it is the tree he has in mind, it is leaning away from the house and would not blow down on the house. He further states that these trees have such a remarkable habit of not dying, he does not think they should be removed until they do die."[7]

The sentry posts used by marines as they stood guard around the president appear small and uncomfortable. *Time* magazine reported in 1935 that the president tried to play a joke on his aide, Lt. Col. Edwin "Pa" Watson. Before leaving for a trip to Chicago, Roosevelt invited Watson to go for a ride. With the president driving, they went around the foundation grounds to the hill where the presidential marine guard stood watch. Pointing, the president told Pa Watson he could use that tent and that they had an army blanket to keep him warm. The colonel held his own by responding, "That's fine. Eighty percent of my service was spent under canvas and I don't see much of it on this White House assignment."[8]

IN 1944, Roosevelt won reelection to the presidency of the United States for a record fourth time, but unknown to almost everyone, his health was beginning to fail. He visited Warm Springs from November 28 to December 17, his longest visit since April 1940. On March 30, 1945, he returned for what would be his final visit to his beloved Warm Springs. Roosevelt came off the train slumped in his wheelchair, lacking his usual enthusiasm and alarming those who had gathered to greet him.

William Hanson reported: "I hadn't seen him for about two years. I was home from the Army and I saw him pass. He looked so bad since the last time I'd seen him. . . . When I returned to Fort Benning, I told my roommate that I saw the President and that he was in bad condition and I didn't think he could live very much longer."[9] Ruth Stevens, a local resident, agreed. When Roosevelt got off the train at the depot, she asked a correspondent, "Honey, is he all right?" The reply: "Tired to death. But he'll pull out of it. He always has."[10]

In this photograph made by Daisy Suckley, he and Grace Tully are shown working on the porch of the Little White House during this last visit. It is one of the very few photos that indicate Roosevelt had leg problems.

THANKSGIVING DINNERS with Roosevelt as the featured speaker were a revered tradition at the Warm Springs Foundation in the late 1920s and 1930s (as illustrated by this photo), but he was an absent guest during most of the war years. Daisy Suckley gave a detailed accounting of his last fall holiday at Warm Springs in her diary. She described the arrival of Roosevelt, Polly Delano, Basil O'Connor, herself, and others at Warm Springs on Tuesday, November 28, 1944. Though it was supposed to be a private trip not announced by the press, there was "quite a crowd at the station. . . . The President drove around the main building where the patients were assembled and clapped and waved and smiled—Up the hill to the Little White House." At the Founder's Dinner, O'Connor presided and sat at the head table with Roosevelt, ambassador Leighton McCarthy, and actress Bette Davis. Davis had been entertaining troops at nearby Fort Benning. Daisy described her: "She looks like a little girl and everyone finds her very nice." She described the audience as well: "It is hard to know who the patients are unless there is a wheelchair or a crutch, etc., for everyone is cheerful and happy looking."[11]

During the visit, Roosevelt suffered several coughing fits. Some guests thought he looked thin and tired at the dinner. He nonetheless sought out the staff to ask: "What I want to know is—are we keeping the best of what we started with, now that we've got all the handsome architecture—the feeling and the spirit?" After the Thanksgiving dinner, Graham Jackson entertained the group with songs, and patients and staff put on a show dedicated to the president titled "The Spirit of Warm Springs." Suckley added that Mr. and Mrs. Cason Callaway and Mr. and Mrs. Louis Haugheys (he served as assistant treasurer at the Warm Springs Foundation) came to tea later in the week, and Lucy Mercer Rutherfurd, Roosevelt's love interest in 1918, also visited.[12]

IN FEBRUARY 1945, Roosevelt flew to the Yalta Conference to meet with Winston Churchill, prime minister of England, and Joseph Stalin, premier of the Soviet Union. They held the secret meeting to plan the postwar reorganization of Europe. Winston Churchill visited Georgia at least twice during the 1930s and 1940s and went to some of the same places as Roosevelt. The prime minister visited Atlanta, where he spoke at Georgia Tech, and Fort Benning but never at the same time as the president.

Roosevelt flew to Yalta on the *Sacred Cow*, the first airplane built specifically for use by the president of the United States. Douglas Aircraft constructed the plane with an elevator, partly to make it easier to help Roosevelt get into the plane since no ramp would be needed for his access. Tifton native and University of Georgia graduate Henry Tift Myers (shown here, far left, with the *Sacred Cow*) served as the pilot.

Ironically, Myers got a phone call while in England in April 1945 that Roosevelt had died. A few hours later, he and Elliott, the president's second son, were in the air headed to Washington, D.C., for the funeral. Myers also flew President Truman in the *Sacred Cow*. Later presidents would use Air Force One for their air travel.[13]

MIKE REILLY, a personal assistant to Roosevelt for many years, approved of Roosevelt's decision to travel to Warm Springs in March 1945. War news from Europe had been good, and "the Boss" needed rest. Reilly later wrote: "We had all seen the Boss come aboard trains bound for Warm Springs looking tired and ill. But when those same trains brought him back to Washington he was always tan and strong and raring to go. . . . Warm Springs had saved his life once, and I always felt he looked upon it as a miraculous source of strength and health. Certainly, it had never failed to wipe out colds, sinus attacks, nerves, or just plain out-and-out physical exhaustion."[14]

Reilly got his first hint of problems when he helped transfer Roosevelt into his car at the Warm Springs depot on March 30. He had done this for over ten years with no difficulty, but suddenly, "he was absolutely dead weight." Reilly had to summon all his strength to complete the transfer.[15] In the course of the next two weeks, however, color returned to Roosevelt's complexion and he got work done. Still, Roosevelt and his doctors knew that he was suffering from congestive heart failure.

On this visit to Warm Springs, Roosevelt was accompanied by friends: former Canadian ambassador Leighton McCarthy; Basil O'Connor; cousins Laura "Polly" Delano and Margaret "Daisy" Suckley; his dog, Fala; and Delano's Scottish terrier, Sister. Laura Delano had been with Roosevelt more than three decades earlier when he first visited Georgia on a trip to Brunswick with the navy. Daisy Suckley later remembered that "when he came on the train in Washington . . . he looked completely exhausted." They arrived in Warm Springs about 1:30 p.m. "Fala was the first off the train and, to create a little excitement, proceeded to get lost for a few minutes in the crowd that had come to greet the President at the station," Suckley recalled. She added, "For a while after reaching the Little White House, the President appeared to be so tired that he would do nothing but sit in a chair with a book in his hands."[16]

As Roosevelt gained strength, the group began to explore the area. Suckley recalled that "the drives were through lovely rolling country . . . the sun comfortably warm under blue skies—so different from the cold bleak days of last December." On one trip, she wanted a snapshot, so she handed the camera to Secret Service agent Jim Beary, who stood on an embankment and took this photo as the car neared. Charles Frederick and chauffeur Monty Synder are riding in the front seat. They traveled north toward Greenville, then west and turned around in Troup County when they reached a wooden bridge not strong enough to support the weight of the car and its passengers. Suckley remembered, "Fala usually lying on the floor, his head on his master's foot; or sitting on the little seat with the wind blowing his shaggy hair out of his eyes."[17]

ROOSEVELT and his companions went to the chapel at the Roosevelt Warm Springs Institute on April 1, Easter Sunday. According to Ruth Stevens, he seemed especially nervous during the service and dropped his hymnal and his glasses. He did not speak to anyone, a contrast to his usual friendly self, as captured in this photograph made at the chapel during the 1938 dedication.[18] Basil O'Connor, who had been visiting, saw him that morning for the last time. Several days later, area residents saw Roosevelt and friends drive through LaGrange and Troup County.

Daisy Suckley remembered the 1945 trip to Warm Springs:

> The first real interruption to this restful schedule came on Thursday, April 5 when President [Sergio] Osmena of the Philippines arrived at 11 in the morning. I remember that it was a cool bracing day. . . . The President gave a very clear statement as to what he intends to do in respect to the Philippines. He was in fine form and looked so much better than a week ago that we almost forgot he was not still his old self. He looked as though he had put on some weight, and his face looked fuller and much less thin. The conference appeared to be without effort or strain.[19]

Many expected that Roosevelt would promise the islands' independence from the United States as an example to the Soviet Union and Great Britain that freedom should be given to "liberated countries."

One day, Laura Delano and Daisy Suckley were reading in the living room of the Little White House while the president worked on his stamp collection. He suddenly looked up and said, "What do you think of this—a simple new stamp without an engraving—on the top line '3 cents 3' on the bottom line 'United States Postage' and, in the middle, 'April 25, 1945. Toward United Nations.'" He called Frank Walker, postmaster general, who was also in Warm Springs, and within the week, as Daisy noted, "A new stamp-issue was born!"[20]

HENRY MORGENTHAU JR., a Hudson River Valley neighbor and secretary of the treasury, arrived in Warm Springs on April 11. He had been in Florida visiting his wife, who was hospitalized, but journeyed to the Little White House to discuss with Roosevelt his plans to publish a book on the German economy. In his diary, he described the visit that evening: "I was terribly shocked when I saw him and I found that he had aged terrifically and looked very haggard. His hands shook so that he started to knock the glasses over, and I had to hold each glass as he poured out the cocktails. . . . I found his memory bad, and he was constantly confusing names."[21]

After dinner (in the Little White House dining room, shown here), the two men discussed the German situation and Morgenthau's belief that the German economy should be kept weak to prevent Germany from gaining political strength after the war. Morgenthau recalled, "I . . . said good-bye to the President and his company, and when I left them they were sitting around laughing and chatting, and I must say the President seemed to be happy and enjoying himself."[22]

ON MONDAY, APRIL 9, Lucy Page Mercer
Rutherfurd joined Roosevelt at Warm Springs. Lucy,
Eleanor's former social secretary, had almost caused the
breakup of the Roosevelts' marriage in 1918. She had since
married and been widowed. She and Roosevelt reestablished
their friendship during the 1920s, exchanging letters and rare
visits over the years. He visited with her at the Rutherfurd
estate in Aiken, South Carolina, and at a friend's home. In
April 1945, she brought with her to Warm Springs artist
Elizabeth Shoumatoff and photographer Nicholas Robbins.
Madame Shoumatoff, a Russian immigrant, had first painted a
portrait of Roosevelt in 1943 in Washington, D.C., also at the
request of Rutherfurd. Robbins took this shot of Roosevelt on
April 12. The effects of polio plus the stress of thirteen years
as president had taken a costly toll on his health.

The next day, Roosevelt sent a message to Prime Minister
Winston Churchill stating: "I would minimize the general
Soviet problem as much as possible, because these problems,
in one form or another, seem to arise every day. . . . We must
be firm, however." He referred to a controversy about Russia
having three votes in the United Nations. Time proved that
Roosevelt made a significant mistake in not telling the public
about this arrangement earlier.[23]

One afternoon during Lucy's visit, she and the president
went for a drive to Dowdell's Knob. Walter Doyle, son of Ed
Doyle, manager of Roosevelt's farm in the 1920s, had just
gotten married, and he and his wife were visiting family members in Warm Springs. He saw a familiar motorcade "with
the Georgia State Patrol leading the way." He recalled, "Mr.
Roosevelt and somebody, I believe it was the lady painting
the portrait [more likely it was Lucy], sitting on the back seat
of the car, followed by the last patrol car. As he passed twenty
feet away, driving slowly down the road, we sat there and

looked at him. I couldn't believe it. His complexion was the
color of ashes. If I've ever seen a dead man propped up on the
back seat of a car, it was him. He looked awful. . . . That was
three days before he died."[24]

During his stay in Warm Springs, Roosevelt worked on his
Jefferson Day speech, which he planned to give during a radio
address on April 13, 1945. On Wednesday, the eleventh, Daisy
Suckley remembered that Roosevelt spent time writing the
speech. The last words offered a guideline for the future: "The
only limit to our realization of tomorrow will be our doubts of
today. Let us move forward with strong and active faith."[25]

ON THE MORNING of April 12, Dr. Howard Bruenn told Daisy Suckley and Laura Delano that the president had a slight headache and a stiff neck. Suckley noted in her diary that Roosevelt came out of his room about noon. "He came in, looking very fine in a double breasted grey suit and crimson tie. His colour was good & he looked smiling & happy & ready for everything. Mme. S [Shoumatoff] exclaimed: 'Mr. President, you look so much better than yesterday, I am glad I did not start working until today.'" She had been sketching every day but had not started the final portrait.[26]

Shoumatoff was in the midst of painting this portrait about 1:00 p.m., when Roosevelt slumped over. He declared he had a terrific headache and never regained consciousness. He was pronounced dead at 3:35 p.m. having suffered a cerebral hemorrhage.[27]

Shoumatoff never touched the famous portrait (shown in the photo) after Roosevelt's death. Several years later, after a call from Atlanta realtor and slum fighter Charles F. Palmer, she gave the portrait to the Little White House, where it remains on display. On the twenty-fifth anniversary of the death of the president, Shoumatoff spoke at a ceremony in Warm Springs. Those in attendance included Graham Jackson, Grace Tully, Frank Allcorn, and Palmer. Shoumatoff stated, "What amazed me most during those hours I spent with him was the fact that the man whom I was immortalizing with my brush was crippled in any way. His alertness, his energy, and interest in everything were always there."[28]

DURING THE APRIL 1945 VISIT, Roosevelt sometimes worked at the Little White House with his legs propped up. Daisy Suckley took this snapshot of the president deep in concentration. Local resident Ruth Stevens recorded the details of Roosevelt's last visit. At the suggestion of Roosevelt's staff, the community planned a barbecue. Warm Springs patients had prepared a special minstrel show, and Stevens baked his favorite nut cake. She reported: "April 12th was to be the greatest day of my life. Think of entertaining the President of the United States!"[29] At 5:00 a.m. on Thursday, Stevens, Jess Long, and Leonard Williams met Warm Springs mayor Frank Allcorn and his wife, lit fires in the barbecue pits, and put two hogs and a lamb on to cook. Hens had been cooked and Brunswick stew, which the president had requested, had been made. Tables were covered with oilcloths and decorated with spring flowers.

The dinner quickly grew from an intimate party to an event for sixty-four. Bun Wright, Reubin Bridges, and others waited to play "Coming 'Round the Mountain" for Roosevelt, just as they had thirteen years earlier when they entertained at the housewarming of the Little White House. By 4:45 p.m., when the president was fifteen minutes late, guests knew something was up. Perhaps Germany had surrendered! Then Maj. Dewitt Greer of the White House Signal Corps Detachment drove up, and his face clearly indicated a problem. He asked that the music be stopped and told the mayor, "Frank, I guess we won't be able to have the party. The Boss is dead."[30]

Long remembered: "When the word came that he was dead everyone was stunned. We just stood there. Old Bun Wright put his fiddle back in its case and said he'd never play it again. That night we brought all the meat and Brunswick stew we had prepared into town and gave it away."[31]

The death of the president shocked the nation. People had put their trust and faith in Roosevelt as he guided them through the Depression and all but the final stages of World War II. Many young people remembered only having one president. The people of Warm Springs perhaps experienced more shock than most. If they had seen him, they had noticed his pale coloring and the dark circles around his eyes, but they fully expected him to recover his spirits and good health, just as he always had in Warm Springs. The *Warm Springs Mirror* noted: "To these people, Franklin Roosevelt was not just a President, but a sincere friend."[32]

AFTER ROOSEVELT DIED, people around the world grieved. In a United Press article, newsman Merriman Smith, who had traveled with the president, reported: "At no time was there any indication that he was sick, beyond the fact that he had not made his usual visits to the Warm Springs swimming pool." He remembered Roosevelt visiting with Osmena: his face looked drawn, "but he did not look or act like a man who was going to die in a week."[33]

He described the nightmare of the evening of April 12. "People were shouting, telephones were ringing, telegraph and typewriters clattered. The Foundation did not want their buildings and spaces overrun by strange reporters and photographers so the three White House correspondents reported the story and wrote all night. The next morning, the reporters joined others to form the procession which traveled from the Little White House to the depot at Warm Springs."[34]

Editors of the *Columbus Enquirer* wrote: "Roosevelt was most certainly a casualty of the war in which all his sons are fighting and in which he had given magnificent leadership. His close attention to the duties of his office during more than 12 years sapped his strength." Indeed, the day after his death, newspapers across the country carried their usual feature "Today's Army-Navy Casualty List." The first entry noted "Roosevelt, Franklin D. Commander-in-Chief."[35]

The *Rome News-Tribune* found reassurance in Roosevelt's death. "Since under the providence of God the time of his departure had arrived, it is fitting that Franklin Delano Roosevelt should quit the scene in the little town of Warm Springs, Georgia which not only symbolizes his humanitarianism but will remain a perpetual reminder of his heroism in facing triumphantly a great physical handicap."[36]

ROBERT COPELAND worked with Roosevelt on his farm for many years. He met Roosevelt several times and recalled that on April 12, 1945, "I was plowing a field in Greenville, Georgia. . . . [Someone] came to the field where I was plowing to tell me the news . . . Mr. Roosevelt died. I just switched the tractor off. . . . I didn't have much spirit in me to plow the balance of the evening cause I felt like I had lost one of the closest friends I had."[37]

Frank Cheatham, who had shaken hands with Roosevelt several years earlier while he was a patient at the foundation, remembered: "I was standing out back of my fraternity house at Athens, the University of Georgia, when a fraternity brother rushed out and said the President is dead. I was stunned. I just could not move. The man I thought was invincible was vulnerable after all."[38]

Georgia governor Ellis Arnall echoed the thoughts of many: "I am shocked beyond words at the news of President Roosevelt's death. There is no calculating the great loss the people of America and the world have suffered with the passing of our wartime leader. President Roosevelt, in a recent conversation with me, said that he had much preferred to return to private life, but that he felt that it was his duty to serve. He died in service, I am sure that is the way he preferred to go."[39]

Eleanor Roosevelt quickly made her way from Washington, D.C., to Warm Springs. Vice Admiral Ross T. McIntire, surgeon general of the navy, and Stephen T. Early, one of Roosevelt's secretaries and closest friends, joined her as she flew to Fort Benning and traveled on to Warm Springs by automobile. They arrived just before midnight on the day that he had died, but Eleanor's long day then only got longer. Polly Delano, a cousin who was with the couple on Roosevelt's first trip to Georgia in 1913, is reported to have told Eleanor that Lucy Mercer Rutherfurd had been there that week. Polly added that daughter Anna had been present at several meetings between Franklin and Lucy. Having been a widow for just a few hours, Eleanor now knew that the woman he had an affair with in 1918 was with him at his death.[40]

The following day, the casket left for Washington, D.C., at 10:00 a.m. Representatives of the armed forces accompanied the hearse on foot as Roosevelt left his beloved foundation and the small town of Warm Springs for the final time. The hearse followed the route that Roosevelt usually took when he left by circling around the campus of the Warm Springs Foundation and made a final stop at the Warm Springs Depot. Patients, some in wheelchairs, and employees of the institute gathered in front of Georgia Hall as the hearse departed.

ACCORDING TO WILLIAM HANSON, a local resident who had seen Roosevelt earlier, "All the services were represented. . . . We were given the order to face the train. . . . Even to the toughest soldier, they had tears running down their cheeks. . . . I don't think there was anybody who didn't feel they had lost a friend." Three thousand soldiers assembled and preceded the hearse from the Little White House to the Warm Springs Depot. The U.S. Army Band from Fort Benning led the procession.[41]

Stationed at Fort Benning when Roosevelt died, Sgt. Harold Luckow, of Fairmont, Minnesota, summed up the reaction of many who thought the death of Roosevelt was "one of the greatest blows to this country—like losing a great battle." He added, "It's like losing your best friend, isn't it?"[42]

VIRGINIA SHIPP remembered everyone being in front of Georgia Hall as "the cortege made a circle right in front of Georgia Hall. . . . It continued down to the Village where the coffin was put in the train. While we were in front of Georgia Hall, Graham Jackson with his accordion played 'Going Home.'" Tears streamed down the musician's face as he played for his president and friend.[43]

Jackson had played for Roosevelt just six months earlier during his November 1944 visit. After Roosevelt's body left Warm Springs for the final time, he continued to play. He later commented:

> I saw everything and I heard every sound and what I heard seemed to mean even more than what I saw. I heard the sighing of the pines and the singing of the mocking bird. . . . Regiments of soldiers had come in during the night. I heard the scraping of their leather boots and the noise of thousands of shifting rifles; the sound of wheels on the gravel and the click of camera shutters.
>
> The hearse came around the small flower-bed in front of Georgia Hall and stopped there a minute, just like he used to pause and wave to the patients as he drove along. It was like his last good-bye. Then the car with Mrs. Roosevelt. I saw her through the glass. . . . It seemed as if she was thinking of everybody else and supporting the whole crowd herself, being so brave. . . .
>
> I glanced to my left at the long line of those poor pitiful people. . . . They were keyed up and so tense. . . . So I lifted my accordion and sounded the opening chords of the Largo of the New World Symphony, and I played Going Home. Surprise, relief and then a look of peace and being comforted seem to come to every face.[44]

Jackson then went inside Georgia Hall and began playing the piano. Patients came in, one by one. Jackson stated: "For two hours I played everything beautiful that came into my head and everybody sat quietly and listened. In the end, I did not seem to feel so terribly sad as I had felt and the others looked as if their hearts were not so heavy."[45]

THE NATIONAL SPOTLIGHT focused on Warm Springs, where servicemen and patients gathered during those days in April 1945. Representatives from the U.S. Army, Navy, Air Force, and Marines stood guard by the body during the trip to Washington, D.C., and Hyde Park, New York, in the same railroad car in which Roosevelt had journeyed to Warm Springs just thirteen days earlier. A window had to be removed so that the casket would fit through the door of the *Ferdinand Magellan*, the armor-plated Pullman car he rode in during most of World War II. Normally, the last car on the train, it was moved to next to last for the funeral train. Hoke S. "Red" Shipp, executive housekeeper at the foundation, and staff carpenter A. G. Moody built a

bier to hold the casket for the train ride. Fittingly, Moody used lumber cut from Georgia pine and grown on foundation property to construct the stand.[46]

A memorial service held at the foundation coincided with services held in Hyde Park. The Sara Delano Roosevelt Community Building served as the site of a Warm Springs memorial service. Those services coincided with those held in the Blue Room of the White House at 4:00 p.m. EWT. Patients, staff, and others who knew Roosevelt attended. George H. Huntington, minister of the Congregational Church and a polio victim, presided. Alice Lou Plastridge, a veteran physiotherapist at Warm Springs, spoke as did Dr. C. E. Irwin, chief surgeon

and medical director, and Fred Botts, a former patient and longtime staff member. The *Warm Springs Mirror* reported: "After a short worship service conducted by Rev. R. W. Greene, Jr., many lingered in prayer and meditation—for this was to them something which touched their very utmost inner spirits. And yet, as they thought of this man, who had been a regular visitor since 1924, they could not forget the characteristic smile, the carefree mood and friendly spirit which had always been exemplified by this association with them."[47] A few months later, residents gathered at the same site to celebrate the successful end of World War II and to remember those who had made the ultimate sacrifice.

Foundation staff members Betty Brown and Hazel Stephens recorded their thoughts in a letter to William George Mackey Davis, chief petty officer with the Seabees in the South Pacific and a relative of Stephens: "The entire service was lovely and left us with the feeling that all of us will do our best to carry out to the best of our ability our individual jobs in order to carry on the great work which he started. Somehow we feel that we were privileged to be associated with this institution at the time we have been. . . . He certainly loved his place. . . . The Little White House where he died will in all probability become a National Shrine."[48]

THE PEOPLE OF Warm Springs and Georgia were left with memories of personal encounters with their president. Evelyn Winchell, a reporter for the *Columbus Ledger*, had known Roosevelt during her childhood in Warm Springs and shared the shock of the nation when he died. In talking about his last train ride out of the town (as documented in the three photographs shown here), she reported: "It was hard for we who knew him . . . to look at the back platform of that train and not see him standing there, as he had always done, with his familiar grin, waving and calling, 'Good-bye, see you again soon,' . . . The love and esteem in the hearts of Meriwether County folks was no superficial hero-worship. He was loved for himself alone, for the affection began when he first came to Warm Springs."[49]

She went on to describe a running gag between the president and his friend Judge Henry H. Revill that contained much truth. Roosevelt would make a joking comment about his public support to which Revill would solemnly reply, "You will please bear in mind that you didn't get anywhere until you came out of the North to Georgia, and then people realized you must have pretty good sense."[50]

She added: "I saw him cry once. It was when his friends in Meriwether made up a contribution to his campaign for Governor of New York. When it was presented to him, he couldn't keep back tears of appreciation, for he recognized on the list names of some he knew weren't really able to contribute but who did because they loved him."[51]

She concluded her article by solemnly stating: "And so Warm Springs and Meriwether . . . watched heart-broken as a friend and fellow citizen, neighbor and loved one . . . went to join the immortals."[52]

Roosevelt loved the people of Georgia, and they loved him and missed him when he was gone.

CHAPTER 7

Lasting Legacy in Georgia

AFTER ROOSEVELT DIED, many people suggested memorials to honor the fallen president. Mayor William Hartsfield of Atlanta sent letters to President Harry Truman and Secretary of State Edward R. Stettinius proposing that Warm Springs "be made the permanent headquarters of the peace organization the world hopes [might] come out of the San Francisco United Nations Conference for International Organization" as a lasting memorial to Roosevelt. In his letter, Hartsfield pointed out the geographic closeness between Warm Springs and transportation and communication connections in Atlanta, adding that "Warm Springs would lend itself to scenic development and still be far away from distractions of large cities."[1]

Mayor F. W. Allcorn Jr. summed up the town's role in memorial plans in a talk to the Warm Springs Woman's Club in October 1945: "This community has been a rather unusual one for many years, with its beautiful natural surroundings and the world fame it gained through that distinguished leader Franklin D. Roosevelt. With all this and the mantle of immortality he placed on Warm Springs when he passed on in our midst, it behooves us to realize our responsibility to make this community what he would have liked it to have been."[2]

Washington columnists speculated that the Little White House (shown in this photograph) would be moved to Hyde Park "brick by brick and board by board." Instead, it became a historic site operated as part of the Georgia Parks and Historic Sites. The foundation became the Roosevelt Warm Springs Institute for Rehabilitation.

In a memorial address on the occasion of the first day of issue of the "Little White House" stamp on August 24, 1945, Basil O'Connor reflected that Roosevelt viewed the Georgia Warm Springs Foundation as "an institution in which those who are patients receive not only the best medical care but also gain from their surroundings, that indomitable courage which he had to refuse to be handicapped in any way by his disease." The Little White House would "remind all people of his love for the common man."[3]

MANY MEMORIALS to Roosevelt can be found around Georgia. In the fall of 1945, Billy Humphries, a fifteen-year-old polio patient, broke ground in front of the depot at Warm Springs. A two-hundred-pound projectile was scheduled to mark the spot where Franklin Roosevelt decided to relaunch his political career in 1928. On Humphries's left in the photograph is Dr. Neil Kitchens, who advised Roosevelt to accept the nomination as governor of New York. The depot was torn down after 1945, but years later a replica was built to house the Warm Springs visitors' center.

The group gathered in front of the "colored" waiting room of the depot. That waiting room serves as a reminder that conditions did not necessarily improve for all residents of Meriwether County or West Georgia during the years that Roosevelt visited. The standard of living for many whites and especially for blacks improved only slightly over the years. The coming of rural electrification, which brought electricity to houses in the area, helped many, but finding good employment and good schools continued to be a challenge.

ROOSEVELT HAD a significant impact on agriculture and farmers. He loved Warm Springs and Georgia and wanted the area to have a secure and prosperous future. Rexford G. Tugwell wrote, "As a private citizen, or even as governor of another state (1924 to 1933), there was nothing he could do in a public way. But he generated the notion that [farmers] might find other crops and save the special way of life he admired so much."[4]

Roosevelt also left a legacy in the South that causes him to be derided periodically. Sometimes referred to as "the vine that ate the South" or as a plague that has always been present, an Asian plant, kudzu (shown in the photo), was promoted as the latest, greatest fast-growing ground cover. In March 1941, operators of Roosevelt Farms at the Georgia Warm Springs Foundation adopted a "Farm Conservation Plan." The first practice listed on the six-page document is "Perennials—Kudzu Field Planting." In 1942, they planted thirty-five acres with kudzu and fifteen acres in 1943. The establishment of practices included the following directions: "The farmer will prepare the land, furnish and apply 400 pounds of 16% superphosphate or its equivalent per acre and give necessary cultivation to establish a satisfactory stand and growth." The Pine Mountain Soil Conservation District would furnish 2,500 kudzu plants for five acres, and the farmer was expected to furnish 22,500 plants to complete the planting. Tap Bennett, supervisor of operations at Pine Mountain Valley, and Roy Durham, farm operator at Roosevelt Farms, signed the plan for the farm.

Both Roosevelt and Cason Callaway considered kudzu an effective ground cover to stop erosion caused by poor farming practices, such as not rotating crops and not adding fertilizers to the soil. Little did they or others realize that the vine would grow so rapidly and take over many fields and forests as it crept across the South in later years.[5]

AS MANY NOTED, Roosevelt was a "nut on trees." He did not want trees cut unless absolutely necessary, and he wanted new trees planted wherever possible. He did this at the Little White House and at his farm on Pine Mountain. He helped create the Civilian Conservation Corp and other agencies that planted trees throughout the South and the nation. Roosevelt encouraged the growth of trees both because he loved the plants and, equally importantly, because he considered growing timber an economically sound idea. When Roosevelt came to Georgia and the South in 1924, much of the land lay barren, the result of farmers growing cotton and other crops without proper rotation or fertilizer use, year after year. On November 28, 1934, he told members of the press in Warm Springs that he had been watching Georgia farmers and the wood products industry. He felt there were many new uses for wood products that would greatly help the southern economy. With his love of trees, Roosevelt helped change the physical appearance of the South. A historical marker erected by the state of Georgia (shown in the photograph) reminds people of Roosevelt's love of trees.[6]

ANOTHER NATIONAL LEGACY of Roosevelt's efforts is the March of Dimes. As Roosevelt said at the November 1935 Thanksgiving dinner at Warm Springs: "For the first time . . . research into one definite known problem is adequately financed and every person, every scientist, who is engaged in this research work has been able to come to this Committee and the Warm Springs Foundation and be given sufficient funds to carry on the work that he is doing." Such concentrated fund-raising and research efforts into curing one disease have since been copied by many groups.[7]

The success of the March of Dimes led to another memorial to Roosevelt, one that millions of people see every day but rarely notice. Soon after his death, the U.S. Treasury Department made plans to introduce a new coin honoring President Roosevelt. First appearing in time for the 1946 March of Dimes kickoff on the president's birthday, the Roosevelt dimes have been minted by the millions every year since 1946.

FRANKLIN ROOSEVELT cared deeply about the South and worried about the economic future of its people. In a July 4, 1938, speech at the Conference on Economic Conditions of the South, he declared: "It is my conviction that the South presents right now the nation's No. 1 economic problem—the nation's problem, not merely the South's. For we have an economic unbalance in the nation as a whole, due to this very condition of the South."[8]

In November 1934, five governors of southern states met with him in Warm Springs to request his help in dealing with the railroads. The railroad rate system in the United States put southern industry at a disadvantage compared to other parts of the country. Finally by 1945, passage of the Interstate Commerce Commission brought an end to the rate differential system for different parts of the country. With that meeting, the group organized what became the Southern Governor's Association, which has eighteen members and seeks to promote the southern region. The men who gathered on November 11, 1934, are shown in this photo: (seated left to right) Eugene Talmadge, governor of Georgia; Olin D. Johnston, governor-elect of South Carolina; President Franklin Delano Roosevelt; (standing, left to right) Ibra C. Blackwood, governor of South Carolina; A. H. Graham, lieutenant governor of North Carolina; D. Bibb Graves, governor-elect of Alabama; and David Scholtz, governor of Florida.

ROOSEVELT LEFT a somewhat mixed legacy with the people of Georgia. He inspired many, he led the nation through the Depression and World War II, but perhaps he could have done more. He left a personal legacy in Georgia with the people he worked with at Warm Springs, met on the roadsides, or visited in places like LaGrange and Pine Mountain Valley. William Winn described his impact on people of the Cove a half century after his death: "To this day, he is remembered fondly, even reverently, by locals, to whom he was part friend, part father figure, and, because of the role he played in pulling the South out of the depression, part savior as well."[9]

Roosevelt wanted much for the people of Georgia. Cason Callaway stated: "His enthusiasm for raising the picture higher on the wall for the people of this section knew no bounds, whether it was for better education, better forestry practices, rural electrification, child welfare, the beauty of the countryside."[10] However, this legacy of being a friend to all, including famous political leaders and poor farmers, may have prevented him from having an even greater impact on Georgia and the South. His wife, Eleanor, along with many black leaders of the day, wanted him to do more about segregation and civil rights in general, but the president seemed unwilling to upset political leaders or the general population. Walter White, a close friend to Eleanor, served as the executive secretary of the National Association for the Advancement of Colored People. White grew up in Atlanta, and his grandmother was from LaGrange. In the decades after Roosevelt died, schools in Georgia and across the nation began to desegregate under federal court orders, and the civil rights movement began to empower African Americans, allowing them to participate more fully in political and economic life in the South. In this 1947 photograph, Eleanor Roosevelt walks with President Harry S. Truman, who succeeded Roosevelt in office, and Walter White of the NAACP.

POLIO BEGAN to be wiped off the world map, thanks to development of vaccines in 1952 by Jonas Salk and in 1955 by Albert Sabin. Salk received a fellowship from the National Foundation for Infantile Paralysis, which Roosevelt had established in 1937. The March of Dimes and research into the cause and treatment of polio continued. The twenty-first century finds the world free of polio in all but a couple of countries. The Global Polio Eradication Initiative, spearheaded by national governments, the Centers for Disease Control and Prevention headquartered in Atlanta, Rotary International, the World Health Organization, and UNICEF, with substantial support from the Bill and Melinda Gates Foundation, leads these efforts. Roosevelt set an example by not letting the disease stop him, and he continues to inspire millions of physically handicapped and able-bodied people. Roosevelt remains the only disabled person ever elected as head of a major nation. In this photograph, Eleanor Roosevelt joins Basil O'Connor (far right), Dr. Albert Sabin (fifth from left), and Dr. Jonas Salk (third from right) at the dedication of the Infantile Paralysis Hall of Fame in Warm Springs on January 2, 1958.

THE MOST ENDURING LEGACY of Roosevelt is the inspiration he has provided not only to residents of Georgia but to millions throughout the world. Though he employed tricks such as walking with his arm hooked through the elbow of a son or an aide to make him appear more at ease and used the national media to promote the image of an active, physically healthy man, Roosevelt struggled daily to overcome handicaps caused by polio. Great strides continue to be made in completely eradicating polio around the world and in overcoming the effects of paralysis, disease, and accidents. Arthur Carpenter expressed his admiration for the president in 1936 when he resigned from his duties at the Georgia Warm Springs Foundation: "It has been a most thrilling experience to see the institution at Warm Springs develop into a well-directed and adequately equipped place for the after-treatment of Infantile Paralysis, and to see the Foundation become the symbolism and instrumentality of a coordinated fight against Infantile Paralysis throughout the country. Through it all I have come to owe an increasing debt of gratitude to [Roosevelt] personally for the example of rising above a physical handicap."[11]

In death, Roosevelt continued to benefit the foundation. In late April 1945, twelve insurance companies paid $560,000 to the foundation as the beneficiary of insurance Roosevelt had taken out in 1930 after he began to devote more time to the political arena than to Warm Springs. The foundation had paid the annual premiums, and the monies were used to continue its work in treating victims of polio.[12]

Dowdell's Knob, the picnic spot Roosevelt first wrote about in a Roosevelt Says column in 1925 and last visited just days before his death, is accessible through the park. A bronze statue of Roosevelt wearing leg braces and sitting on a car seat has graced the spot since 2007. The Georgia Department of Natural Resources commissioned the statue, which Atlanta sculptor Martin Dawe created. This tribute to Franklin Delano Roosevelt at his favorite picnic spot plus the Little White House and several historical markers help Georgians remember that in the mid-twentieth century, a New York native who became the longest-serving president in United States history considered Georgia his second home.

APPENDIX   Developments at the Little White House and Roosevelt Warm Springs Institute

Adapted from *The Roosevelt Warm Springs Institute for Rehabilitation Commemorates the 100th Anniversary of the Birth of Franklin D. Roosevelt, 1882–1982.*

1893   The Meriwether Inn is built by Charles T. Davis.

1923   George Foster Peabody, president of the Warm Springs Corporation, takes over the operation of the resort.

1924   Franklin Delano Roosevelt first visits Warm Springs.

1926   Roosevelt buys the resort with two-thirds of his own capital. Donald Ross, the "Father of American Golf Course Architects," is commissioned by Roosevelt to build an eighteen-hole golf course.

Dr. LeRoy Hubbard of New York comes to Warm Springs to conduct a study to determine the benefits of water therapy. He monitors twenty-three patients. All benefit from the therapy, and the American Orthopedic Association approves of the treatment.

Helena Mahoney, the first physical therapist, begins working under the guidance of Dr. Hubbard.

1927   Roosevelt deeds the property to the newly incorporated Georgia Warm Springs Foundation. It treats sixty-one patients the first year.

1928   The first physical therapist from Peabody College, Nashville, Tennessee, arrives. By 1930, the staff has increased to eleven physiotherapists.

Mr. and Mrs. Edsel Ford present the new glass-enclosed pool to the foundation.

1930   The Norman Wilson Infirmary is built with funds raised by patients and their friends and named for a young Philadelphia patient who died shortly after he left Warm Springs.

1932   Roosevelt builds his Little White House.

1933   Roosevelt is inaugurated as president of the United States.

Over three hundred men and women, representing sixty thousand Georgia donors, present Georgia Hall to President Roosevelt during a dinner on November 24. Cason Callaway and Cator Woolford lead the effort.

1934   The first Birthday Balls are held throughout the land.

1935   Kress Hall is built with funds largely donated by Samuel H., Rush H., and Claude W. Kress

The Hageman-Harris Company, of New York City, and a group of material and supply contractors finance the construction of Builders Hall.

1937   The chapel, which is principally a donation of Georgia Wilkins, one of the former owners of the Meriwether Inn and Springs, opens.

1938   The National Foundation for Infantile Paralysis is organized.

The brace shop comes into being.

1939   The school and library, a gift of Mrs. S. Pinkney Tuck, is completed.

The Medical Building, a complete orthopedic hospital, opens, greatly improving medical care and treatment.

The Sara Delano Roosevelt Community House in Warm Springs is officially dedicated. Constructed with funds from the Works Progress Administration, the building actually opens in 1937.

1941   The physical and occupational therapy graduate course is developed to train therapists in the specialized care of polio patients.

1942   The campus pool is completed.

1945   President Roosevelt dies at the Little White House.

Public pools close.

1946   The new east wing is added to the medical building for a total bed capacity of 141.

1951   Psychological and social services are added to the patient care program.

1953   Roosevelt Hall, a long-projected rehabilitation center and auditorium, is built with the help of the National Foundation for Infantile Paralysis.

The recreation building (clubhouse) is built for staff recreation activities.

1954   The Salk vaccine, developed through research supported by the National Foundation for Infantile Paralysis, helps erase the scourge of polio.

1956   Founders Hall is erected.

1964   The Georgia Rehabilitation Center is dedicated to providing vocational rehabilitation services to disabled Georgians.

1974   On July 4, the hospital complex and lands are conveyed to the State of Georgia by the Georgia Warm Springs Foundation.

1980   Governor Busbee dedicates the newly renovated pools and springs and announces the new mission of the Roosevelt Warm Springs Institute for Rehabilitation.

1981   An extensive renovation program is initiated, which leads to the modernization and beautification of existing facilities and grounds.

1996   Ruzycki Center for Therapeutic Recreation opens.

2007   Blanchard Hall opens. The hall houses vocational rehabilitation.

2011   The student dorm opens.

McCarthy Cottage burns.

NOTES

Introduction

1. Asbell, *FDR Memoirs*, 249.

CHAPTER 1. Discovering Warm Springs and Georgia

1. "Roosevelt Says," *Macon Telegraph*, May 2, 1925.
2. *Brunswick News*, November 16, 1913, 1.
3. FDR Master Speech File, Remarks to Orthopedic Surgeons Visiting Warm Springs, Georgia, December 7, 1935, Franklin and Eleanor Roosevelt Papers, FDR Library, Hyde Park, N.Y., hereafter referenced as "FDR Library."
4. FDR Speeches File, November 29, 1934, FDR Library.
5. FDR Personal Correspondence Files, October 24, 1924, 1920–28, FDR Library
6. Elliott Roosevelt, *FDR*, 1:566–67.
7. Dallek, *Foreign Policy*, 1979.
8. *Macon Daily Telegraph*, January 14, 1925, 4.
9. Presidential Press Conferences, November 23, 1934, FDR Library.
10. Freidel, *FDR and the South*, 8.
11. Anderson, *Wild Man from Sugar Creek*, 125.

CHAPTER 2. Fighting Polio

1. Tobin, *Man He Became*, 172; $500,000 Insurance Policy, FDR Library.
2. Tugwell, Warm Springs Oral History Interviews, FDR Library, hereafter cited as "Tugwell Interviews."
3. Gallagher, *FDR's Splendid Deception*, 40; *Columbus Ledger*, October 17, 1925.
4. Rhoads, "Franklin D. Roosevelt"; Elliott Roosevelt, *FDR*, 1:620–21; FDR Speeches Files, March 24, 1937, FDRLibrary.
5. Ibid., 70.
6. Tugwell Interviews.
7. Franklin Roosevelt, Family, Business & Personal Papers, 1925, box 61, FDR Library.
8. Ibid.
9. J. E. Smith, *FDR*, 215.
10. Joseph Lash, *Eleanor and Franklin*, 296.
11. Elliott Roosevelt, *FDR*, 1:617.
12. *Meriwether Vindicator*, May 14, 1926, 2.
13. Paul Hasbrouck Collection, Letters from Warm Springs, April 8–May 11, 1927, FDR Library.
14. Ibid.
15. Ibid.
16. *Atlanta Journal*, October 3, 1928, 8.
17. FDR Speeches File, June 4, 1929; Dec. 7, 1935; FDR Library.
18. *Franklin Roosevelt: Poor Man's Friend*.

19. William Trotter, interview by author, November 9 and November 30, 1998.

20. *Franklin Roosevelt: Poor Man's Friend*.

21. Gallagher, *FDR's Splendid Deception*, 40.

22. Veeder Scrapbooks and Tapes, Roosevelt Warm Springs Institute.

23. Lindley, *Franklin D. Roosevelt*, 212.

24. *Warm Springs Advertiser*, December 5, 1930.

25. Elliott Roosevelt, *FDR*, 1:163–64.

26. Rollins, *Roosevelt & Howe*, 203–4; *Atlanta Georgian*, November 7, 1926, 5.

27. Tugwell Interviews.

28. *Atlanta Journal*, October 3, 1928.

29. *Atlanta Journal*, February 26, 1927, 2.

30. Tugwell Interviews.

31. Hasbrouck Collection, letter April 10, 1927, FDR Library.

32. Ibid.

33. FDR Speeches File, 1929, FDR Library.

34. Tugwell Interviews.

35. *Meriwether Vindicator*, April 24, 1925, 3.

36. Bishop, *FDR's Last Year*, 536.

37. President's Secretary's Files, box 136, FDR Library.

38. William Trotter, interview by author, November 9 and 11, 1998.

39. *I Remember Roosevelt*, 1999.

40. FDR Speeches File, November 23, 1939, FDR Library.

41. *Manchester Star-Mercury*, April 19, 1995, 4, letter to editor.

42. Tugwell Interviews.

43. FDR Speeches File, May 9, 1934, November 28, 1935, FDR Library.

44. President's Secretary's Files, FDR Library

45. Ibid.

46. FDR Speeches File, November 26, 1931; November 29, 1934, FDR Library.

47. Harmon, *Warm Springs Story*, 127.

48. FDR Speeches File, FDR Library.

49. *Warm Springs Mirror*, July 28, 1933, 2.

50. FDR Speeches File, FDR Library.

51. Rhoads, "Franklin D. Roosevelt," 81.

52. *Franklin Roosevelt: Poor Man's Friend*.

53. *I Remember Roosevelt*, 1998 and 1999.

54. Perkins, *Roosevelt I Knew*, 77.

55. Eleanor Roosevelt, *This I Remember*, 28.

56. *Waycross Journal Herald*, November 21, 1933.

57. President's Secretary's Files, box 136; FDR Speeches File, November 29, 1934, both in FDR Library.

58. FDR Speeches File, FDR Library.

59. *Franklin Roosevelt: Poor Man's Friend*.

60. *Meriwether Vindicator*, April 7, 1939, 2.

61. Presidential Correspondence, FDR Library.

62. Eleanor Roosevelt, *This I Remember*, 85.

63. Hershan, *Woman of Quality*, 233–34.

64. Tugwell Interviews.

65. Ibid.

66. Tugwell Interviews.

67. President's Personal Files, Wilkins, FDR Library.

68. FDR Speeches File, November 30, 1933, FDR Library.

69. Rosenman, *Working with Roosevelt*, 394–95.

70. *Atlanta Constitution*, April 13, 1945.

71. Tugwell Interviews.

72. *I Remember Roosevelt*, 1999.

73. Harmon, *Warm Springs Story*, 93, 98; N. Rogers, "Race."

CHAPTER 3. An Active Man

1. *Columbus Ledger*, October 22, 1924.

2. Huff, "Clifford Walker."

3. Harmon, *Story of Warm Springs*, 41.

4. *Americus Times-Recorder*, February 6–8, 1928.

5. Ibid.

6. Ibid.

7. *LaGrange Reporter*, March 4, 1927, 1.

8. *I Remember Roosevelt*, 1999.

9. Freidel, *FDR and the South*, 9.

10. Tugwell Interviews, Warm Springs Interview Summary.

11. *I Remember Roosevelt*, 1998.

12. *Atlanta Constitution*, September 27, 1928.

13. FDR Speeches File, 1926–1928, FDR Library.
14. Burke and Burke, *Images of America*, 59.
15. *Columbus Ledger*, October 2, 1928, 1.
16. *Columbus Enquirer*, October 5, 1928.
17. Worsley, *Columbus on the Chattahoochee*.
18. *Meriwether Vindicator*, November 9, 1928.
19. Rosenman, *Working with Roosevelt*, 29.
20. *New York Times*, December 3, 1928, 3; December 4, 1928, 4.
21. Rosenman, *Working with Roosevelt*, 29.
22. FDR Speeches File, FDR Library.
23. Ibid.
24. *Carrollton County Times*, May 9, 1929, 1.
25. Persico, *Franklin and Lucy*, 170–72.
26. Myrtice Chauncey, interview by author, October 2, 2000.
27. Kuhn, Joye, and West, *Living Atlanta*, 62.
28. Martin, *William Berry Hartsfield*, 174.
29. Tugwell Interviews.
30. FDR Speeches File, May 9, 1929, FDR Library.
31. Ibid.
32. Ickes, *Secret Diary*, 1:127.
33. *Franklin Roosevelt: Poor Man's Friend*.
34. *LaGrange Daily News Graphic*, December 4, 1930.
35. *Warm Springs Advertiser*, November 21, 1930.
36. Ruth Stevens, *"Hi-Ya Neighbor,"* 32.
37. *Atlanta Journal*, October 13, 1931.
38. *Columbus Enquirer*, October 13, 1931.
39. *Columbus Ledger*, October 14, 1931, 1, 7.
40. *Columbus Sunday Ledger-Enquirer*, October 11, 1931, 15.
41. *Atlanta Journal*, December 9, 1931.
42. *Atlanta Journal*, December 4, 1931.
43. *Atlanta Journal*, December 10, 1931.
44. *Warm Springs Mirror*, February 28, 1932.
45. Robert Carpenter, interview by author, November 30, 1998.
46. Tugwell Interviews.
47. *Roosevelt: Poor Man's Friend*.
48. Ibid.
49. Ibid.
50. Ibid.
51. Anna R. Halsted Oral History Interview, 24, FDR Library.
52. Oral History Project, Special Collections, Georgia State University, Atlanta.
53. Eleanor Roosevelt, *This I Remember*, 28.
54. Lindley, *Franklin D. Roosevelt*, 28.
55. FDR Family, Business, and Personal Papers, October 18, 1930, FDR Library.
56. Howell, "Georgia Warm Springs Foundation," 8.
57. Tugwell, "Episode below Dowdell's Knob," 78.
58. Interview with T. J. Long by William S. Kirkpatrick, 1953, Tugwell Papers, FDR Library.
59. Goodwin, *Franklin D. Roosevelt's Plan*.
60. *Meriwether Vindicator*, December 12, 1930.
61. *Meriwether Vindicator*, December 2, 1932.
62. February 21, 1934, letter to Herman Swift, Warm Springs, President's Secretary's Files, FDR Library.
63. Martha Tigner, interview with author, March 3, 1998.
64. Ibid.
65. Ibid.
66. Stevens, *"Hi-Ya, Neighbor,"* 38.
67. Martha Tigner, interview with author, March 3, 1998.
68. *Atlanta Journal*, November 30, 1931.
69. McDuffie, Small Collection; Elliott Roosevelt, *FDR*, 2:839; Janken, *White*, 226.
70. Lippman, *Squire of Warm Springs*, 88.
71. Oral History Interviews, Georgia State University, Atlanta.
72. Martha Tigner, interview with author, March 3, 1998; *Roosevelt: Poor Man's Friend*.
73. Correspondence between Fred Botts and FDR, in PPF Files 311, FDR Library.
74. *Atlanta Journal*, March 24, 1932, 1.
75. *Atlanta Journal*, May 1, 1932.
76. *Warm Springs Mirror*, May 6, 1932.
77. *Roosevelt: Poor Man's Friend*.
78. *Meriwether Vindicator*, May 13, 1932, 1.
79. Perkins, *Roosevelt I Knew*, 80.

80. PSF Warm Springs, box 136, FDR Library.

81. Grieve, "Work That Satisfies."

82. Tugwell, *Democratic President*, 219.

83. FDR Speeches File, FDR Library.

84. *Savannah Morning News*, July 1, 1932, 3.

85. Vogt, "Richard B. Russell."

86. M*eriwether Vindicator*, October 28, 1932, 1.

87. Ibid.

88. Letter in the possession of Robert Carpenter.

89. *Atlanta Journal*, October 25, 1932; *Atlanta Constitution*, October 25, 1932.

90. Freidel, *FDR and the South*, 2.

91. *Atlanta Journal*, October 25, 1932.

92. Perkins, *Roosevelt I Knew*, 112.

93. Oral History Interviews, Georgia State University, Atlanta.

94. FDR Speeches File, October 24, 1932, FDR Library.

95. *Atlanta Constitution*, October 25, 1932.

96. *Tifton Gazette*, October 28, 1932, 6; March 3, 1933, 1; March 10, 1933, 4.

97. Williams, *History of Tift County*, 102–3.

98. Holmes, "From Euphoria to Cataclysm," 327.

99. *Roosevelt: Poor Man's Friend.*

100. Ibid.

101. Tugwell Interviews.

102. Robert Carpenter, interview with author, November 30, 1998.

103. Tugwell Interviews.

104. Eleanor Roosevelt, *This I Remember*, 27.

105. Eleanor Roosevelt, "Appreciation from Mrs. Roosevelt."

CHAPTER 4. Leading the Nation

1. *Warm Springs Mirror*, March 25, 1932, 1.

2. Holmes, "From Euphoria to Cataclysm," 327.

3. *Meriwether Vindicator*, November 6, 1936, 1; *Warm Springs Mirror*, November 6, 1936, 1.

4. *Meriwether Vindicator*, July 29, 1938, 1.

5. *Warm Springs Mirror*, March 25, 1932, 1; November 6, 1936; November 8, 1940, 1.

6. FDR Speeches Files, FDR Library.

7. *Warm Springs Mirror*, December 11, 1931.

8. William Trotter, interview with author, November 9, 1998.

9. Reprinted in *Warm Springs Mirror*, March 10, 1933.

10. President's Personal Files, Botts, FDR Library.

11. FDR Speeches File, FDR Library.

12. *Savannah Morning News*, November 19, 1933.

13. Ibid.

14. *Savannah Morning News*, November 17, 1933, 1.

15. Georgia Senate Journals, 1935, 65; *Warm Springs Mirror*, January 17, 1936, 2; *Atlanta Journal*, November 29, 1935.

16. FDR Speeches File, FDR Library.

17. *Cordele Dispatch*, November 20, 1933, 1.

18. FDR Speeches File, FDR Library.

19. FDR's Presidents Secretary's Files, Warm Springs, FDR Library.

20. FDR Speeches File, November 18, 1933, FDR Library.

21. Tully, *FDR*, 66.

22. *Warm Springs Mirror*, December 11, 1936, 2.

23. Oral History Program, Georgia State University, Atlanta.

24. *Meriwether Vindicator*, December 8, 1933, 4; *Warm Springs Mirror*, November 30, 1933, 1.

25. *Warm Springs Mirror*, December 7, 1934.

26. Interview by Gary M. Fink, February 17, 1987, Georgia Government Documentation Project, Special Collections, Georgia State University.

27. Ibid.

28. *I Remember Roosevelt*, 1998.

29. Walker, *Roosevelt*, 161.

30. Stevens, *"Hi-Ya, Neighbor,"* 53.

31. FDR Speeches File, December 7, 1935, FDR Library.

32. *Warm Springs Mirror*, January 26, 1934, 2.

33. Walker, *Roosevelt*, 237.

34. H. H. Callaway, *Story of a Man*, 13–14.

35. Freidel, *FDR and the South*, 19–20.

36. *LaGrange Daily News*, November 22, 1935, 1.

37. *Atlanta Journal*, November 29, 1935, 1.

38. *Time*, December 9, 1935, 16.

39. Trips of the President Files, September–October 1935.

40. Ibid.

41. *Warm Springs Mirror*, December 6, 1935, 3.

42. FDR Speeches File, November 29, 1935, FDR Library.

43. *Time*, December 9, 1935, 16.

44. Walker, *Roosevelt*, 237.

45. William Trotter, interview with author, November 9, 1998.

46. FDR Speeches File, March 31, 1938, FDR Library.

47. *Atlanta Journal*, December 3, 1935.

48. Conkin, "It All Happened," 20.

49. *Warm Springs Mirror*, May 3, 1940, 1.

50. Winn, "Pine Mountain Valley," in *New Georgia Guide*.

51. Conkin, "It All Happened," 29; Skinner, "I Remember Roosevelt," 69–70.

52. Walker, *Roosevelt*, 208.

CHAPTER 5. Tougher Times in Georgia

1. Tugwell Interviews.

2. FDR Speeches File, FDR Library.

3. *Atlanta Constitution*, March 19, 1937.

4. FDR Speeches File, March 18, 1937, FDR Library.

5. President's Personal Files, University of Georgia file, FDR Library.

6. Ward, *Closest Companion*, 78.

7. http://www.millercenter.org/blog/presidential-leadership-and-disaster-politics.

8. *Gainesville Eagle*, April 16, 1936.

9. *Toccoa Record*, March 24, 1938, 1.

10. FDR Speeches File, March 23, 1938, FDR Library.

11. Ibid.

12. *Time*, April 4, 1938, 10.

13. Freidel, *Franklin D. Roosevelt*, 283.

14. *Meriwether Vindicator*, March 25, 1938, 1.

15. *Griffin Daily News*, March 24, 1938, 1.

16. FDR Speeches File, March 23, 1938, FDR Library.

17. FDR Speeches File, March 30, 1938, FDR Library.

18. *Columbus Ledger-Enquirer*, March 30, 1938, 1.

19. FDR Speeches File, November 29, 1934, FDR Library.

20. *Celebrating Our Heritage* video.

21. J. Roosevelt and Libby, *My Parents*, 121.

22. *I Remember Roosevelt*, 1998.

23. *Athens Banner-Herald*, August 11, 1938.

24. Ibid.

25. FDR Speeches Files, August 11, 1938, FDR Library.

26. *Athens Banner-Herald*, August 11, 1938.

27. Gurr, *Personal Equation*, 171.

28. FDR Speeches Files, August 11, 1938, FDR Library.

29. Russell Papers, Speeches, Barnesville File, Russell Library, University of Georgia, Athens.

30. Ibid.

31. *Atlanta Constitution*, August 10, 1938.

32. President's Personal Files, Official Files, August 2, 1938, FDR Library.

33. FDR Master Speech Files, August 11, 1938, FDR Library.

34. *Time*, August 22, 1938, 19.

35. *Barnesville News Gazette*, August 25, 1938.

36. Zeigler, "Senator Walter George's 1938 Campaign," 351.

37. *Time*, August 22, 1938; President's Personal Files, Official Files, August 2, 1938, FDR Library.

38. *Meriwether Vindicator*, September 16, 1938, 2.

39. Talmadge, *Political Legacy*, 40.

40. Eleanor Roosevelt, *This I Remember*, 7.

41. Russell Papers, Political File, Lamar County, Russell Library, University of Georgia, Athens.

42. Ibid.

43. *LaGrange Daily News*, November 23, 1938.

44. Elliott Roosevelt, *FDR*, 2:830.

45. Egerton, *Speak Now against the Day*, 120.

46. *LaGrange Daily News*, November 29, 1938.

47. *Meriwether Vindicator*, September 22, 1939.

48. Elliott Roosevelt, *FDR*, 2:830–31.

49. Wither, *President Travels by Train*, 388.

50. Sherwood, *Roosevelt and Hopkins*, 114–15.

51. *LaGrange Daily News*, April 24, 1940.

52. *Atlanta Journal*, April 19, 1940, 1.

53. *Warm Springs Mirror*, November 24, 1939.

54. Mary Ellen Hill, interview with author, January 21, 2015.

55. FDR Speeches Files, November 29, 1941, FDR Library.

56. White, *FDR and the Press*.

57. *Time*, December 2, 1935.

58. *Macon Evening News*, November 24, 1939, 1.

59. *Time*, December 9, 1935, 14.

60. Ickes, *Secret Diary*, 1:239.

CHAPTER 6. Commander in Chief

1. FDR Speeches File, November 23, 1939, FDR Library.

2. *Atlanta Journal*, April 20, 1943.

3. Ward, *Closest Companion*, 210.

4. Ibid., 211.

5. FDR Speeches Files, April 15, 1943, FDR Library.

6. Ward, *Closest Companion*, 211–12.

7. President's Personal File, 1-I, FDR Library.

8. *Time*, December 16, 1935, 15.

9. *Franklin Roosevelt: Poor Man's Friend*.

10. Walker, *Roosevelt and the Warm Springs Story*, 186.

11. Ward, *Closest Companion*, 348.

12. Ibid., 347–48.

13. Cella, *Fixing the Moon*, 60–61.

14. Reilly, *Reilly in the White House*, 225–26.

15. Ibid., 227.

16. Tugwell Interviews, FDR Library.

17. Ibid.

18. Ibid.; Bishop, *FDR's Last Year*, 566.

19. Tugwell Interviews, FDR Library.

20. Ibid.

21. Blum, *Roosevelt and Morgenthau*, 628.

22. Ibid., 630.

23. FDR to Churchill, April 1945, Map Room Papers, FDR Library,.

24. *I Remember Roosevelt*, 1998.

25. Tugwell Interviews.

26. Ward, *Closest Companion*, 417.

27. Ibid., 419.

28. Shoumatoff, *FDR's Unfinished Portrait*, 133.

29. Stevens, *"Hi-Ya, Neighbor,"* 89.

30. Ibid., 89–91.

31. Tugwell Interviews, FDR Library.

32. *Warm Springs Mirror*, April 20, 1945, 1.

33. *Atlanta Constitution*, April 13, 1945.

34. Ibid.

35. *Columbus Enquirer*, April 13, 1945.

36. *Rome News-Tribune* April 13, 1945; photo of front-page headline in *LaGrange Daily News*, April 13, 1945.

37. *Roosevelt: Poor Man's Friend*.

38. Ibid.

39. *Newnan Herald*, April 19, 1945, 5.

40. Persico, *Franklin and Lucy*, 345.

41. *Roosevelt: Poor Man's Friend*.

42. *Atlanta Constitution*, April 13, 1945.

43. *Roosevelt: A Poor Man's Friend*.

44. Jackson Collection, April 19, 1945, Atlanta History Center.

45. Ibid.

46. Asbell, *When FDR Died*, 127.

47. *Warm Springs Mirror*, April 20, 1945, 1.

48. W. W. Rogers, "Death of a President," 119.

49. *Columbus Ledger-Enquirer*, April 15, 1945, 1.

50. Ibid.

51. Ibid.

52. Ibid.

CHAPTER 7. Lasting Legacy in Georgia

1. *Warm Springs Mirror*, June 15, 1945.
2. *Warm Springs Mirror*, October 5, 1945, 1.
3. Warm Springs Foundation, Papers of Stephen Early, FDR Library.
4. Tugwell, "Episode below Dowdell's Knob," 72.
5. Mart A. Stewart, "Kudzu," New Georgia Encyclopedia, 2002, 2014.
6. Presidential Press Conferences, November 28, 1934, FDR Library.
7. FDR Speeches File, November 28, 1935, FDR Library.
8. Franklin D. Roosevelt: "Message to the Conference on Economic Conditions of the South," *The American Presidency Project*, http://www.presidency.ucsb.edu/ws/?pid=15670.
9. *New Georgia Guide*, 361.
10. Schubert, *Cason Callaway of Blue Springs*, 55.
11. President's Secretary's Files, Warm Springs, June 27, 1936.
12. *Newnan Herald*, April 26, 1945, 9.

BIBLIOGRAPHY

Primary Sources

Atlanta History Center, Atlanta, Georgia.
    Jackson, Graham, Collection.
    Shepperson, Gay Boling, Papers.

Berry College, Special Collections, Rome, Georgia.
    Berry, Martha, Papers.

Chipley Historical Society, Pine Mountain, Georgia.
    Celebrating Our Heritage, the Chipley-Pine Mountain Story
        Produced by Lee Davis, 1998. Videocassette (VHS).
    Civilian Conservation Corps scrapbooks.

Franklin D. Roosevelt Presidential Library, Hyde Park, New York.
    Hasbrouck, Paul, Collection.
    McDuffie, Lizzie, Remembrances in Roosevelt Small Collections.
        Reminiscences by Contemporaries, 1920–1962.
    Roosevelt, Franklin and Eleanor, Papers. "Little White House
        Historic Site, Warm Springs, Georgia."
    Tugwell Collection, Rexford G. Tugwell Warm Springs Oral History
        Interviews. Includes interviews with Daisy Bonner, Mr. and Mrs.
        Lee Rowe, Daisy Suckley, Rev. W. G. Harry, and others.

Franklin D. Roosevelt State Park, Warm Springs, Georgia.
    Goodwin, George. *Franklin D. Roosevelt's Plan for Developing Warm
        Springs, Georgia.* Report of Findings in Twenty-One Interviews.
        Conducted by Goodwin for the Franklin D. Roosevelt Warm
        Springs Memorial Commission, 1950.
    I Remember Roosevelt. Video recordings of oral presentations
        held at the Little White House Museum, August 22, 1998–
        August 21, 1999.

Georgia Department of Archives and History, Atlanta.
    Vanishing Georgia Photo Collection.

Pullen Library, Special Collections, Georgia State University, Atlanta.
    Georgia Government Documentation Project.
    Carter, Jimmy. Interview by Gary M. Fink, February 17, 1987.
    Mackay, James. Interview by Cliff Kuhn, March 18, 1986.
    Musgrove, Downing. Interview by Jane W. Herndon,
        August 11, 1971.
    Pendergrast, Nan. Interview by Nasstrom and Cliff Kuhn,
        June 24, 1992.

Roosevelt Warm Springs Institute Library, Warm Springs, Georgia.
    Veeder, Mary Hudson. Scrapbooks and tapes.
    Whitehead, Lynn Pearson, Scrapbook.

Russell Library, University of Georgia Libraries, Athens.
    Russell, Richard, Collection.

Troup County Archives, LaGrange, Georgia.
    Callaway, Cason/Callaway Gardens Papers.
    Callaway, Fuller E., Collection.
    Nix-Price Collection.

Newspapers
....

Americus Times-Recorder
Athens Banner-Herald
Atlanta Constitution
Atlanta Georgian
Atlanta Journal
Barnesville News-Gazette
Brunswick News
Carroll County Times
Columbus Enquirer
Columbus Ledger
Columbus Ledger-Enquirer
Fitzgerald Herald
Gainesville Eagle
Griffin Daily News
Hogansville Home News
LaGrange Daily News
Macon Evening News
Macon Telegraph
Manchester Star-Mercury
Meriwether Vindicator
Newnan Herald
Rome News-Tribune
Savannah Evening Press
Savannah Morning News
Tifton Gazette
Toccoa Record
Warm Springs Advertiser and Warm Springs Mirror

Interviews by Author
....

Carpenter, Robert. November 30, 1998.
Chauncey, Myrtice. October 22, 2000.
Daniel, Joe. November 6, 1998.
Hudson, Charles D. November 6, 1998.
Page, Gene. July 16, 1998.
Tigner, Martha. March 3, 1998.
Trotter, Bill. November 9 and 30, 1998.
Wilkes, Johnny. October 22, 1998.
Yates, Charles R. Interview by Philip Cleaveland for author,
    April 3, 2000.

Secondary Sources
....

Anderson, William. *The Wild Man from Sugar Creek: The Political
    Career of Eugene Talmadge*. Baton Rouge: Louisiana State University
    Press, 1975.
Asbell, Bernard. *The FDR Memoirs*. Garden City, N.Y.: Doubleday,
    1973.
————. *When FDR Died*. New York: Holt, Rinehart, and Winston,
    1961.
Barfield, Louise Calhoun. *History of Harris County, Georgia, 1827–
    1961*. Columbus, Ga.: Columbus Office Supply, 1961.
Berger, Mark L. "Franklin D. Roosevelt and Cason J. Callaway: An
    Enduring Friendship." *Georgia Historical Quarterly* 79, no. 4
    (Winter 1995): 904–19.
Beschloss, Michael R. *Kennedy and Roosevelt: The Uneasy Alliance*.
    New York: W. W. Norton, 1980.
Bishop, Jim. *FDR's Last Year, April 1944–April 1945*. New York:
    William Morrow, 1974.
Blum, John Morton. *Roosevelt and Morgenthau*. Boston: Houghton,
    Mifflin, 1970.
Brands, H. W. *Traitor to His Class: The Privileged Life and Radical
    Presidency of Franklin Delano Roosevelt*. New York: Doubleday,
    2008.

Burke, David M., Jr., and Odie A. *Images of America: Warm Springs*. Charleston, S.C.: Arcadia, 2005.

Callaway, Howard H. *The Story of a Man and a Garden: Cason Callaway and Callaway Gardens*. New York: Newcomen Society of North America, 1965.

Carter, Jimmy. *An Hour before Daylight: Memories of a Rural Boyhood*. New York: Simon and Schuster, 2001.

Caudle, O. R. "A Reality." Troup EMC edition of *GEMC: Georgia* (Official Publication of the Georgia Electrical Membership Corporation) 50, no. 6 (June 1994): 17.

Cella, Bonne Davis. *Fixing the Moon: The Story of the First Presidential Pilot and Aviation Pioneer, Lt. Col. Henry Tift Myers*. Macon: Henchard Press, 2005.

Cobb, James C. "The Big Boy Has Scared the Lard out of Them." *Commentary* 43, no. 2 (June 1975): 123–26.

———. "Not Gone, but Forgotten: Eugene Talmadge and the 1938 Purge Campaign." *Georgia Historical Quarterly* 59, no. 2 (Summer 1975): 198–209.

Conkin, Paul K. "It All Happened in Pine Mountain Valley." *Georgia Historical Quarterly* 47, no. 1 (March 1963): 1–42.

Dallek, Robert. *Franklin D. Roosevelt and American Foreign Policy, 1932–1945*. New York: Oxford University Press, 1979.

Egerton, John. *Speak Now against the Day: The Generation before the Civil Rights Movement in the South*. New York: Alfred A. Knopf, 1994.

Fite, Gilbert C. *Richard B. Russell, Jr.: Senator from Georgia*. Chapel Hill: University of North Carolina Press, 1991.

Fleming, Douglas L. "The New Deal in Atlanta: A Review of the Major Programs." *Atlanta Historical Journal* 30, no. 1 (Spring 1986): 23–45.

Flynn, John T. *The Roosevelt Myth*. Garden City, N.J.: Garden City Publishing, 1948.

Franklin Roosevelt: Poor Man's Friend. GAB Productions, 1995. Interviews and production by B. J. Schaffer, Shiloh, Georgia. Videocassette (VHS).

Freidel, Frank. *FDR and the South*. Baton Rouge: Louisiana State University Press, 1965.

———. *Franklin D. Roosevelt: A Rendezvous with Destiny*. Boston: Little, Brown, 1990.

Gallagher, Hugh Gregory. *FDR's Splendid Deception*. New York: Dodd, Mead, 1985

Gellman, Irwin F. *Roosevelt and Batista: Good Neighbor Diplomacy in Cuba, 1933–1945*. Albuquerque: University of New Mexico Press, 1973.

Golay, Michael. *America 1933: The Great Depression, Lorena Hickok, Eleanor Roosevelt, and the Shaping of the New Deal*. New York: Free Press, a division of Simon and Schuster, 2013.

Goodwin, Doris Kearns. *No Ordinary Time: Franklin and Eleanor Roosevelt; The Home Front in World War II*. New York: Touchstone, a division of Simon and Schuster, 1995.

Gregory, Cleburne. "Franklin Roosevelt Will Swim to Health." *Atlanta Journal*, October 26, 1924, p. 7.

Grieve, Victoria M. "Work That Satisfies the Creative Instinct." *Winterthur Portfolio* 42, no. 2/3 (2008): 165.

Gurr, Charles Stephen. *The Personal Equation: A Biography of Steadman Vincent Sanford*. Athens: University of Georgia Press, 1999.

Harmon, F. Martin. *The Warm Springs Story, Legacy & Legend*. Macon, Ga.: Mercer University Press, 2014.

Hershan, Stella K. *A Woman of Quality: Eleanor Roosevelt*. New York: Crown, 1970.

Holmes, Michael. "From Euphoria to Cataclysm: Georgia Confronts the Great Depression." *Georgia Historical Quarterly* 58, no. 3 (1974): 313–30.

Howell, Clark, Jr. "Georgia Warm Springs Foundation and the Little White House." *Southern Magazine*, Georgia Number, 1, no. 7 (October–November 1934): 8.

Hudson, Paul Stephen. "A Call for 'Bold-Persistent Experimentation': FDR's Oglethorpe University Commencement Address, 1932." *Georgia Historical Quarterly* 77, no. 2 (Summer 1994): 361–75.

Huff, Christopher. "Clifford Walker." *New Georgia Encyclopedia*, May 13, 2013. http://www.georgiaencyclopedia.org.

Ickes, Harold L. *The Secret Diary of Harold L. Ickes*. Vol. 1, *The First Thousand Days, 1933–1936*. New York: Simon and Schuster, 1954.

Janken, Kenneth Robert. *White: The Biography of Walter H. White, Mr. NAACP*. New York: New Press, 2003.

Kennedy, Joseph P. *I'm for Roosevelt*. New York: Reynal and Hitchcock, 1936.

Klara, Robert. *FDR's Funeral Train*. New York: Palgrave, Macmillan, 2010.

Kuhn, Clifford M., Harlon E. Joye, and E. Bernard West. *Living Atlanta: An Oral History of the City, 1914–1948*. Athens: University of Georgia Press, 1990.

Lash, Joseph. *Eleanor and Franklin*. New York: W. W. Norton, 1971.

Lindley, Ernest K. *Franklin D. Roosevelt: A Career in Progressive Democracy*. New York: Blue Ribbon Books, 1931.

Lippman, Theo. *The Squire of Warm Springs: FDR in Georgia, 1924–1945*. Chicago: Playboy Press, 1977.

Martin, Harold H. *William Berry Hartsfield: Mayor of Atlanta*. Athens: University of Georgia Press, 1978.

McMahon, Kevin J. *Reconsidering Roosevelt on Race*. Chicago: University of Chicago Press, 2004.

Minchew, Kaye Lanning. "Shaping a Presidential Image: FDR in Georgia." *Georgia Historical Quarterly* 83, no. 4 (Winter 1999): 741–57.

———. "Warm Springs." *New Georgia Encyclopedia*. December 6, 2002. http://www.georgiaencyclopedia.org.

The New Georgia Guide. Athens: University of Georgia Press, 1996.

Perkins, Frances. *The Roosevelt I Knew*. New York: Viking Press, 1946.

Persico, Joseph E. *Franklin and Lucy*. New York: Random House, 2008.

Reilly, F. R., as told to William J. Slocum. *Reilly in the White House*. New York: Simon and Schuster, 1947.

Rhoads, William B. "Franklin D. Roosevelt and the Architecture of Warm Springs." *Georgia Historical Quarterly* 67, no. 1 (Spring 1983): 70–87.

Rogers, Naomi. "Race and the Politics of Polio, Warm Springs, Tuskegee, and the March of Dimes." *American Journal of Public Health* 97, no. 5 (May 2007): 784–95.

Rogers, William Warren, Jr. "The Death of a President, April 12, 1945: An Account from Warm Springs." *Georgia Historical Quarterly* 75, no. 1 (Spring 1991): 106–20.

Rollins, Alfred B., Jr. *Roosevelt and Howe*. New York: Alfred A. Knopf, 1962.

Roosevelt, Eleanor. "An Appreciation from Mrs. Roosevelt." *Southern Magazine*, Georgia Number, 1, no. 7 (October–November 1934): 3.

———. *This I Remember*. New York: Harper & Brothers, 1949.

Roosevelt, Elliott, ed. *FDR: His Personal Letters*. Vol. 1, *1905–1928*. New York: Duell, Sloan and Pearce, 1948.

———, ed. *FDR: His Personal Letters*. Vol. 2, *1928–1945*. New York: Duell, Sloan and Pearce, 1950.

Roosevelt, Franklin D. "Georgia for Winter Warmth! The Governor of New York Relaxes in the Empire State of the South." *Holiday*, February 1931, 7–8.

———. "Message to the Conference on Economic Conditions of the South." July 4, 1938. Presented online by Gerhard Peters and John T. Woolley, *The American Presidency Project*. http://www.presidency.ucsb.edu/ws/?pid=15670.

Roosevelt, James, and Bill Libby. *My Parents: A Differing View*. Chicago: Playboy Press, 1976.

Roosevelt Warm Springs Institute for Rehabilitation Commemorates the 100th Anniversary of the Birth of Franklin D. Roosevelt, 1882–1992. Brochure. 1992.

Rosenman, Samuel I. *Working with Roosevelt*. New York: Harper and Brothers, 1952.

Rowley, Hazel. *Franklin and Eleanor: An Extraordinary Marriage*. New York: Farrar, Straus, and Giroux, 2010.

Schubert, Paul. *Cason Callaway of Blue Springs*. Hamilton, Ga., 1964.

Sherwood, Robert E. *Roosevelt and Hopkins: An Intimate History*. New York: Harper and Brothers, 1948.

Shoumatoff, Elizabeth. *FDR's Unfinished Portrait*. Pittsburgh: University of Pittsburgh Press, 1990.

Skinner, W. Winston. "I Remember Roosevelt." *Folk and Kin Folk of Harris County* 1, no. 1 (Spring 1976): 68–70.

Smith, Jean Edward. *FDR*. New York: Random House, 2007.

Smith, Merriman A. *Thank You, Mr. President: A White House Notebook*. New York: Harper and Brothers, 1946.

Stevens, Ruth. *"Hi-Ya, Neighbor."* New York: Tupper and Love, 1947.

Talmadge, Herman E., and Mark Royden Winchell. *Talmadge: A Political Legacy, a Politician's Life*. Atlanta: Peachtree, 1987.

Tobin, James. *The Man He Became: How FDR Defied Polio to Win the Presidency*. New York: Simon and Schuster, 2013.

Tugwell, Rexford G. *The Democratic Roosevelt*. Garden City, N.Y.: Doubleday, 1957.

———. "Episode below Dowdell's Knob: II." *Center Magazine*, September 1968, 72–80.

———. *In Search of Roosevelt*. Cambridge, Mass.: Harvard University Press, 1972.

Tully, Grace. *FDR: My Boss*. New York: Charles Scribner's Sons, 1949.

Vogt, Sheryl B. "Richard B. Russell." *New Georgia Encyclopedia*. January 15, 2015. http://www.georgiaencyclopedia.org

Walker, Turnley. *Roosevelt and the Warm Springs Story*. New York: A. A. Wyn, 1953.

Ward, Geoffrey C., ed. *Closest Companion: The Unknown Story of the Intimate Friendship between Franklin Roosevelt and Margaret Suckley*. Boston: Houghton Mifflin, 1995.

———. *A First-Class Temperament: The Emergence of Franklin Roosevelt*. New York: Harper and Row, 1989.

White, Graham J. *FDR and the Press*. Chicago: University of Chicago Press, 1979.

Williams, Ida Belle. *History of Tift County*. Macon: Tift County Historical Society, J. W. Burke Co. Printers, 1948.

Winfield, Betty Houchin. *FDR and the News Media*. Urbana: University of Illinois Press, 1990.

Withers, Bob. *The President Travels by Train: Politics and Pullmans*. Lynchburg, Va.: TLC, 1996.

Worsley, Etta Blanchard. *Columbus on the Chattahoochee*. Columbus, Ga.: Columbus Office Supply, 1951.

Zeigler, Luther Harmon, Jr. "Senator Walter George's 1938 Campaign." *Georgia Historical Quarterly* 43, no. 4 (December 1959): 333–52.

ILLUSTRATION CREDITS

INDEX